# NURTURING CHILDREN
# IN THE LORD

**A study guide for teachers on developing a biblical
approach to discipline**

## Jack Fennema, Ed.D.

PRESBYTERIAN AND REFORMED PUBLISHING CO.
Phillipsburg, New Jersey
1980

To Marian

# Contents

# Acknowledgments

A heartfelt thank you must be said first of all to my Heavenly Father for allowing me to have the enjoyable and sometimes tiring experience of writing this book.

Appreciation is extended to several professors who as a doctoral committee accepted "biblical discipline" as a valid dissertation topic within a secular university. They are: Paul Halverson, Brian Lindsey, Alex Perrodin, and Paul Torrance.

A sense of deep gratitude goes to persons who reviewed a rough draft of the book and provided many helpful comments. They are: Dave Fennema, Phil and Joanne Jacquart, Diane Dockery Kelly, Miriam MacNair, Ken Steensma, Rich and Geraldine Steensma, Trevor Tristram, and John Vanderhoek.

No book could be written without typists, thus a thank you is extended to Wendy Ribecca, Clara Fennema, Nancy Fennema, and Elly Groen.

Finally, my family must be acknowledged as being a great source of insight, encouragement, and strength. Nancy, Jeff, and Doug are truly partners in this effort. Thank you.

J.E.F.

# Foreword

This book is the product of a twofold concern. The first concern is over the apparent lack of distinctively biblical approaches to discipline on the market. The best-selling books on Christian discipline over the last several years have often adopted either the behaviorist's or the humanist's approach, added a few proof texts, and labeled it as Christian. There is a real danger in making the Bible fit what appears to be true and/or workable. Such a synthesis often causes Christians to lose a distinctive perspective of life and the world. In this book I have attempted to begin with Scripture to determine patterns for the nurture that God wants for his children. The book has its limitations, I am sure. Each of us has difficulty breaking free from the influence of the patterns of thought from the world around us. But, an honest effort has been made to listen to what God is saying in his Word about nurture and admonition.

This book attempts to avoid "tricks of the trade" or easy solutions to what are often difficult problems. That may be disappointing to some. But the book is meant to be a *study guide,* not a handbook. It is meant for persons who desire to begin thinking through the matter of nurturing children in the Lord. Nurturing or disciplining children is, perhaps, the most difficult and complex task a teacher or parent faces. And that is precisely why there are no easy answers. Children are very complex, and so is the process of introducing them to the truth. It is my contention that many problems in the school and home can be avoided by operating upon a biblically accurate view of the child and creating learning experiences and relationships that are personally and eternally meaningful for the child. If it is true that God created both the child and the world, and I believe that it is, certainly the Word of God can give direction on how to understand and relate the two. It can provide direction and answers for which the secular educator and psychologist can only guess or stumble across. These directives, if interpreted in a manner which properly reflects the mind of Christ, are able to stand side by side with the theories of the secularist and not be found wanting.

The second concern relates more to the people for whom the book is written than to the treatment of the topic. The book is written primarily for the Christian teacher. This includes the pre-service teacher within a Christian college or a public university who may be preparing for a career in teaching. The book is designed to at least supplement certain textbooks used within education courses, but there is a hope that it may supplant certain secular materials as well. The intended audience also includes the in-service teacher. Whether it be used in personal or communal study, a book such as this can easily be the focal point of in-service education within a school.

The book is designed, then, primarily for the Christian pre-service or in-service teacher who is seeking ways to relate his faith to his studies or profession. There can be no dichotomy between the sacred and the secular for the Christian. *All* of life has religious connotations. My desire is that this book can help Christian professionals see that one's studies and one's calling can take on true and full meaning only when they are based on and integrated through Jesus Christ.

But there is a secondary audience for whom this book is written— the non-Christian. So many atheists and agnostics seem to turn off to God because they perceive Christian expression as being either simplistic or irrelevant. My hope is that well-educated non-Christians will be able to read this book and find a reasonable and academically acceptable approach to a very important matter.

References are made throughout the book to Christian schools. Christian day schools are, in my judgment, a necessary avenue for the nurturing of God's children, and it is the Christian teacher within the Christian school who can, perhaps, gain the most from the ideas presented here. But I hope that my colleagues within the public school can also benefit from this publication. There are very few materials on bookshelves today that provide an alternative to the thinking of the behaviorist and the humanist. Options to these positions should be available to *all* professional educators, no matter what their religious persuasion or area of service.

In conclusion, my prayer for this work is that of the Psalmist: "Let the words of my mouth and the meditation of my heart be acceptable in thy sight, O LORD, my rock and my redeemer" (Ps. 19:14).

## Chapter 1

# A Biblical View of the Child

One of the most difficult and yet most important aspects of biblical discipline is that of understanding the nature of children and then acting on that knowledge. This aspect is often not dealt with as much as it should be within the Christian school and home. A great deal of thought is usually given to the instruction of God's children. Christian teachers and parents have always sought to instruct their children in the truth, in the ways of the Lord. God is recognized as the Source and Creator of all truth; in fact, God *is* the Truth. Christian schools instruct children about reality, which has been created by God. Christian homes instruct children in the truth, which originates with God. God has always been acknowledged as the source of instruction for biblical nurture.

But children, too, are created by God. Their origin is the same as that of the created reality in which they are instructed. Truth, reality, and children all originate from the same Source. This fact has great significance for Christian teachers and parents. Not only should they be looking to God and his Word for guidance on the instruction which is to be provided, but they must also look to God's Word to understand the children for whom the instruction and correction is intended. Since reality and children were created by God, they are meant to interact and interrelate in a harmonious manner. Often, however, Christian instruction is emphasized without taking a close look at the child. Little concern is given to the nature of the child, and for that reason conflict and disharmony often result. The beauty of being one with the Lord is that a person *can* have an "inside track" on how things really are, how God really intended them to be. Christians have unique access to the understandings necessary to instruct children.

The nature of reality and the nature of children can be truly understood only by the redeemed in the Lord.

One of the difficulties of nurturing children is that they are such
complex beings, each different from the next. This chapter attempts
to deal with that complexity. Understanding the child is necessary
for the instructing, correcting, and admonishing of the child. Then
the nurturing process can become more personally meaningful to the
child and much more enjoyable for the teacher.

This chapter deals first of all with four basic truths about the child
which must be recognized, accepted, and acted upon by Christian
teachers before they can deal effectively with their children in a manner
which finds harmony with Scripture. They are as follows: 1. The child
is created by God. 2. The child is an image-bearer. 3. The child is a
sinner. 4. The child can be a new creature in Christ. The words
"can be" in the fourth statement have tremendous significance. You
see, all children are created by God, all children are image-bearers,
and all children are sinners. That is true of children in all schools and
in all families. But not all children are new creatures in Christ. They
*can* be; and to be able to possess a lifestyle which is acceptable to
God and man, they *must* be. Only one Person can provide the insight
and power to act in a responsible manner before God and man, and
that is the Person of Jesus Christ.

The final two parts of the chapter speak of the child and motivation and of the child and learning. No one has yet said the final word
on these complex issues, but attempts are made to share insights
which are believed to be in harmony with biblical principles.

### The Child Is Created by God

The Bible is quite plain about the origin of man. Genesis 1:27
states: "So God created man in his own image, in the image of God
created he him; male and female created he them." This fact has several
implications for the manner in which adults are to view children.

### A. As a Religious Being

Genesis 1:27 states that the child is created in the very image of
God, a truth which is dealt with further in this chapter. But Genesis

2:7 records another fact which illustrates man's religious nature: "then the Lord formed man of dust from the ground, and breathed into his nostrils the breath of life; and man became a living being." God breathed into man and gave him life! What significance that one statement holds! God, not man, gives life. God made man to be a living soul. Man was created by design, not by chance, and given the spark of life by the sovereign God. Children continue to breathe the breath which God has given. Children are totally religious beings!

The view of children being totally religious is not accepted within secular schools. At best, the child is acknowledged as being *partly* religious, as having a portion of his life which functions in a spiritual way. The logical implication of this theory is that certain times of the day or week are devoted to spiritual things and the rest of one's time is free for himself or secular pursuits. The same can be said for possessions or activities. Only certain possessions or activities belong to God; the rest belong to man to do with as he pleases. This sacred-secular dichotomy is a false dichotomy and promotes Christian tokenism. Each child is *totally religious*. Each thought, word and action contains religious significance. He is either responding in thankfulness and obedience to his Creator, or he is, in essence, worshiping another.

Because he is a religious being, each child possesses an intrinsic desire to worship. Only man *can* worship, and all men *do* worship. Anthropologists have often said that all societies have worshiped either the true God, another human being, or a part of creation. No one told them to; they possessed the felt need to worship which is intrinsic to man's nature. He was created with that desire, and he is directed to act upon that desire in a God-honoring manner. I Corinthians 10:31 directs that ". . . whatever you do, do all to the glory of God."

The fact that man possesses an intrinsic drive to worship means that there are no secular portions to the Christian's life, his school, or his home. The Christian school does not simply add biblical studies to a secular curriculum. Rather, God is acknowledged as the Source of all which is true and real as one studies each of the disciplines. The same is true within the Christian home. Every activity and relationship comes under the lordship of Jesus Christ. The response of the child to this truth is to be a worshipful response. The child is a totally religious being, and for the Christian child, all of life is a religious experience to be directed towards his Creator Father.

## B. As a Creature

The child is not autonomous. He is dependent rather than independent. He is finite rather than infinite. He is the creature of the Creator God. This is an important point, because the central difference between behavioristic, humanistic, and biblical views of the child is that the first two look to man for answers and the third looks to God.

The child does not gain his identity or personhood from himself, others, or from his actions. He is the crown of creation, endowed with many talents and gifts through God's sheer goodness. Psalm 139:13 quotes David's response to God: "For thou didst form my inward parts, thou didst knit me together in my mother's womb." The King James Version continues in verse 14 with "I will praise thee; for I am fearfully and wonderfully made: marvelous are thy works; and that my soul knoweth right well."

One of the implications of man's creaturely dependence is that all persons are viewed as being equal before God. Man was created equal and remains equal. The Bible states:

> They have all gone astray, they are all alike corrupt; there is none that does good, no, not one (Ps. 14:3).

> For God shows no partiality. All who have sinned without the law will also perish without the law, and all who have sinned under the law will be judged by the law (Rom. 2:11-12).[1]

Another implication of man's creaturely dependence is that there are absolutes. In fact, his Creator is the ultimate Absolute. Man is not the center of the universe. The child is not the center of his experience, his school, or his home. He does not function for his own purposes. He must recognize that there is a God. There is an outside Force to whom he must respond. There are absolutes, ab-

1. Also see Acts 10:34.

solutes which are meant for his well-being and against which he is held accountable. Children are not to look *inward* for the ultimate answers to life. They are not to look *outward* on the horizontal plane either. They are to look *upward* to God in a dependent and creaturely way.

## C. As One Who Is Unique

Each child is different from the next. And he is meant to be different. God could have created each child to be the same as the next, but he chose not to. Teachers are wise to acknowledge and act on this fact.

The biblical concept of "diversity within unity" is an important one for Christian teachers to think through. For one thing, it states that diversity is not bad in itself, and that it is a rather normal and acceptable way to view people, actions, and creation. But diversity without basic unity can lead to chaos and anarchy. One must always begin with unifying principles or truths and then allow flexibility and diversity within that framework.

The Bible speaks often about the uniqueness and diversity of man. Paul states in I Corinthians 7:7 that ". . . each has his own special gift from God, one of one kind and one of another." Romans 12:4-8 also deals with the varying gifts of people. Christ in the parable of the talents spoke about people being dealt with "each according to his ability" (Matt. 25:15). And I Corinthians 12 provides a clear description of the variety of gifts and the concept of diversity within a basic unity.

Each child is created as one who is unique. Each has unique talents, characteristics, and traits. Caution must be exercised against dealing with all children in the same manner. Efforts towards creating conformity of appearance or behavior must take into account the fact that each child has been created as one who is unique. Allowing for the uniqueness within the unity of Christ (Col. 1:17) and his Word is often difficult, but it is biblically necessary.

### The Child Is an Image-Bearer

Genesis 1:27 records that "God created man in his own image."

Other verses support this and further support the fact that, even after the Fall, man continues to bear evidences of the image of God:

> Whoever sheds the blood of man, by man shall his blood be shed; for God made man in his own image (Gen. 9:6).
>
> . . . he is the image and glory of God . . . (I Cor. 11:7).
>
> With it [the tongue] we bless the Lord and Father, and with it we curse men, who are made in the likeness of God (James 3:9).

Volumes have been written on man as image-bearer of God. Man has wrestled with the meaning and implications of that truth for centuries. It would appear that the complexity and the impossibility of fully comprehending the topic reflects a God who is infinitely complex and incomprehensible by finite man. Nevertheless, feeble attempts at understanding have been made which can be shared.

Bearing the image of God must be dealt with in two phases. First, attention must be given to man's task and functions. Secondly, man's nature can be described.

## A. In Tasks and Functions

### 1. The Task of an Image-Bearer

What is the purpose for man's existence? What task has he been given to do? The Westminster Larger Catechism seems to capture the essence of this matter in its first question and answer:

> *Question:* What is the chief and highest end of man?
>
> *Answer:* Man's chief and highest end is to glorify God, and fully to enjoy him forever.

The essence of Scripture gives credence to this statement:

> For from him and through him and to him are all things. To him be glory for ever. Amen (Rom. 11:36).
>
> So, whether you eat or drink, or whatever you do, do all to the glory of God (I Cor. 10:31).[2]

Man was created to bring glory to the Creator! The great commandments found in Matthew 22:37-39 reflect this:

---

2. Also see Psalm 73:24-26; John 17:22, 24; Revelation 19:1.

. . . you shall love the Lord your God with all your heart, and with all your soul, and with all your mind. This is the great and first commandment. And a second is like it, you shall love your neighbor as yourself.

These commandments of love provide an overarching structure within which all other commandments fall. It is the summary of all God's laws.

Although God's Word, the Bible, provides many directives which specifically speak to man's task in this world, there are two which focus on the key dimensions of that task—the Great Commission and the cultural mandate.

The Great Commission, given by Christ and recorded in Matthew 28:19-20, states:

Go therefore and make disciples of all nations, baptizing them in the name of the Father and of the Son and of the Holy Spirit, teaching them to observe all that I have commanded you.

The words "observe all that I have commanded you" lead quite naturally back to the cultural mandate found in Genesis 1:28:

And God blessed them, and God said to them, "Be fruitful and multiply, and fill the earth and subdue it; and have dominion over the fish of the sea and over the birds of the air and over every living thing that moves upon the earth."

Genesis 2:15 elaborates on this mandate: "The Lord God took the man and put him in the garden of Eden to till it and keep it."

The cultural mandate answers an interesting question: What task did God give to man at the beginning of time? What is man to be busy doing? The answer is that man is to serve as a vice-regent in charge of God's creation. He must care for it and not exploit it. Creation's possibilities are to be opened up through cultural development. Man's task is to unearth the riches of creation and bring them into the service of man for the glory of God.

Man's task, then, remains the same as it has always been. But since the Fall, the task has been expanded. One must first experience the restoration found in Jesus Christ before he can live a life of service to God. That is an eternally important fact to remember, since teaching children about service and cultural development without first (or simultaneously) teaching children about the Good News in Christ is to teach works redemption. It is "holding the form of religion but denying the power of it" (II Tim. 3:5).

The commandments of love, the Great Commission, and the cultural mandate all serve as context for the functions of an image-bearer. This context then, summarized briefly, calls for a life of responsive service to God and to one's fellow man.

## 2. The Functions of an Image-Bearer

The functions of an image-bearer reflect the three functions of Christ. He was ordained of God the Father and anointed with the Holy Spirit to be our chief Prophet, our only High Priest, and our eternal King.

Although one function may appear to predominate on a particular occasion, the three always function together as a supportive unity.

a. *Prophethood:* Reflecting God's knowledge

(1) Jesus is the Prophet who reveals God's Word to us.

Concerning Jesus of Nazareth, who was a prophet mighty in deed and word before God and all the people (Luke 24:19).

In the beginning was the Word, and the Word was with God, and the Word was God. . . . No one has ever seen God; the only Son, who is in the bosom of the Father, he has made him known. . . . When the people saw the sign which he had done, they said, "This is indeed the prophet [like Moses] who is to come into the world!" (John 1:1, 18; 6:14).[3]

(2) The prophetic function of man is to *know* (to accept God's revelations of his truth) and then to share this knowledge with others.

Earnestly desire the spiritual gifts, especially that you may prophesy. . . . If a revelation is made to another sitting by, let the first be silent. For you can all prophesy one by one, so that all may learn and all be encouraged (I Cor. 14:1, 30-32).

For I [Paul] would have you know, brethren, that the gospel

---

3. Also see Deuteronomy 18:15-22.

which was preached by me is not man's gospel. For I did not receive it from man, nor was I taught it, but it came through a revelation of Jesus Christ (Gal. 1:11-12).

b. *Priesthood:* Reflecting God's reconciliation of sinners

(1) Jesus is the Reconciler or High Priest through whom we are at peace with God and with one another.

> For if while we were enemies we were not reconciled to God by the death of his Son, much more, now that we are reconciled, shall we be saved by his life. Not only so, but we also rejoice in God through our Lord Jesus Christ, through whom we have now received our reconciliation (Rom. 5:10-11).

> For it is witnessed of him, "Thou art a priest for ever, after the order of Melchizedek" [Ps. 110:4]. . . . Consequently he is able for all time to save those who draw near to God through him, since he always lives to make intercession for them (Heb. 7: 17, 25).[4]

(2) The priestly function of man is to *intercede.* He is a mediator, a facilitator, one who brings a person together with God, other people, and creation. He attempts to resolve conflicts. He is a peacemaker, a healer.

> I therefore, a prisoner for the Lord, beg you to lead a life worthy of the calling to which you have been called, with all lowliness and meekness, with patience, forbearing one another in love, eager to maintain the unity of the Spirit in the bond of love (Eph. 4:1-3).

> For every high priest chosen from among men is appointed to act on behalf of men in relation to God. . . . He can deal gently with the ignorant and wayward, since he himself is beset with weakness (Heb. 5:1-2).[5]

c. *Kingship:* Reflecting God's perfect rule

(1) Jesus is the King who reigns over all.

> He will be great, and will be called the Son of the Most High; and the Lord God will give to him the throne of his father David, and

---

4. Also see Ephesians 2:13-17; I John 2:1-2.
5. Also see Exodus 32:30; II Corinthians 13:11; II Timothy 2:24-25.

he will reign over the house of Jacob for ever; and of his kingdom there will be no end (Luke 1:32-33).

To the King of ages, immortal, invisible, the only God, be honor
and glory for ever and ever. Amen (I Tim. 1:17).[6]

(2) The kingly function of man is to *administer* the world God has
created.

Then God said, "Let us make man in our image, after our likeness; and let them have dominion over the fish of the sea, and over
the birds of the air, and over the cattle, and over all the earth
. . ." (Gen. 1:26).

. . . thou has made him little less than God, and dost crown him
with glory and honor. Thou has given him dominion over the
works of thy hands; thou hast put all things under his feet . . .
(Ps. 8:5-6).[7]

Before a teacher or a child can rightly function as a prophet,
priest, and king, he must first deal with himself in each of these
three areas. Before he can function as a prophet, he must possess
self-knowledge. Before he can function as a priest, he must possess
self-surrender. Before he can function as a king, he must possess self-
control. All must be gained from the Father, through the Son, by the
power of the Spirit.

## B. In Nature

Man as image-bearer was given a *task* by God. He also *functions*
in a particular way as he seeks to carry out that task. But in addition
God has equipped man with a *nature* that allows him to fulfill his
task. Man, as image-bearer, is given certain characteristics, certain
abilities, which assist him to obediently pursue his task. Man in his
nature reflects God; that is, man, in a finite, dependent, and con-
ditioned sense, reflects what God is infinitely, independently, and absolutely. Five such reflective characteristics are dealt with here. No
doubt an infinite God is reflected in many more ways in man, but
the five mentioned have special significance for the instruction, correction, and admonition of children.

---

6. Also see Psalm 9:7-9; Revelation 17:14.
7. Also see Romans 13:1; II Corinthians 13:10; Ephesians 5:21.

## 1. The Child Is a Unity

He is one—body and soul. He is more than an accumulation of parts or characteristics, as the behaviorist might wish to say. He is a *gestalt,* a whole who is greater than the sum of his parts or characteristics. He has meaningful structure through the interrelationship and interdependence of his various parts. The analogy of one body with many parts is used in I Corinthians 12. The child is at once a rational, emotional, spiritual, physical, and social being.

One cannot pull apart the personality of God. All of his traits exist at the same time—his justice, love, holiness, righteousness, etc. Take the ultimate act of God, the gift of his Son. Included in that act are God's love, anger, justice, holiness, righteousness, faithfulness, grace, mercy, patience, wisdom, goodness, sovereignty—all at one and the same time. His is an integrated personality. The same is true for each child as an image-bearer of God (II Pet. 1:3-8). The child exists as a total, unified, integrated person. His physical actions are related to and dependent on his emotional and rational dimensions. His social actions most assuredly interrelate with his physical and emotional dimensions as well. As mentioned previously, all thoughts, words, and actions of the child also possess spiritual connotations. In their dealings with their children, Christian teachers must reflect this holistic, unified view of the child.

## 2. The Child Is Rational

He seeks a logical and orderly environment within which to live. His actions have purpose as he sets goals for his life and works towards meeting those goals. He possesses the ability to think and to understand. He possesses an intellect.

Not only is the child rational, but he seeks to perceive rationality within the world around him. Genesis 1 tells how God took an earth that was without form and void and brought harmony and purpose out of chaos. Man's mind demands that the world be organized. It seeks to discover the patterns and structure of created reality. It attempts to bring order to situations in which none is perceived. This quest after order, system, rationality, is evidenced in one of Adam's first tasks, that of naming the animals. "The man gave names to all cattle, and to the birds of the air, and to every beast of the field . . ." (Gen. 2:20).

### 3. The Child Is Interactive

The child is always in relationship. He is in relationship to God— a relationship which has either become whole through Christ or remains broken because of an unrepentant heart. He is also in relationship to others and to the natural creation. The child reflects a God of relationships. God is triune. He is in relationship as the Father, the Son, and the Holy Spirit. Not only is God in relationship within the Trinity, he also establishes relationships with his creatures. He is an interactive God, one who relates in a personal way; he is a God who communicates.

The child, too, is interactive. He initiates actions and responds with actions. This actional dimension of the nature of the child is viewed differently by behaviorists and extreme humanists. The behaviorist would claim that the child is passive and can only react to stimulation outside of himself. The extreme humanists (Jean Jacques Rousseau in *Emile;* A. S. Niell in *Summerhill*), on the other hand, believe that the child is essentially active and that he initiates all of his actions. He is viewed as being autonomous and independent.

But the biblical view of the child is that he is interactive. That does not mean, however, that he initiates his relationship to God. That is pure grace—God reaching out to man by way of his Son, Jesus Christ, through the activating power of the Holy Spirit. But, the child has an interactive and social dimension to his nature. He is responsible; he has freedom to choose; he is accountable.

### a. *The Child Is Responsible*

He has been given a task. He has responsibilities. He is one who has been called for a purpose. James 1:22 instructs us to be "doers of the word, and not hearers only." The child is to know the truth, and the child is called to act upon or respond to the truth. But not only has he been given a task, a responsibility, he has also been given the ability to carry out that task. As one who is responsible, he is able to respond.

### b. *The Child Has Freedom to Choose*

God gave man a task and he gave man the ability to carry out that task. The task is to be performed as a worshipful response to one's Creator. But this response is to be uniquely his, not one which has been programmed by another. Responses are not to be elicited or drawn from a child in a purely stimulus-response fashion. The child is to be given the opportunity to emit or volunteer unique and original responses.

God created man with freedom to choose; he is not a puppet pulled by strings; he is not a passive being, unable to take the initiative. Adam and Eve in the garden of Eden are the classic examples of freedom of choice, and they chose freely to disobey God. Even today, fallen man retains some freedom of choice. Several Scripture passages speak to this fact:

> And if you be unwilling to serve the LORD, choose this day whom you will serve, whether the gods your fathers served in the region beyond the river, or the gods of the Amorites in whose land you dwell; but as for me and my house, we will serve the LORD (Josh. 24:15).

> Behold, I stand at the door and knock; if any one hears my voice and opens the door, I will come in to him and eat with him, and he with me (Rev. 3:20).[8]

The biblical view of freedom differs, however, from the humanist's. To be free according to the humanist is to be self-determining, wholly directed from within. Only God is free in this sense. Man is a creature and has limitations. Man must function within structure, within the nature he has been given. He does not gain freedom by seeking to be God. He does not find freedom through a lifestyle which denies who he is before God. He finds true freedom through submission to Jesus Christ and the norms found in Scripture (I Cor. 7:22; Gal. 5:1; I Pet. 2:16). This acceptance of structure places man in har-

---

8. Also see John 7:17; Revelation 22:17.

mony with his nature, the world, and his Creator. The concept of "freedom found within submission (servanthood) and structure" is a fundamental premise for a biblical approach to discipline (I Cor. 9:10).

### c. *The Child Is Accountable*

He is responsible; he has freedom to choose; and he is personally accountable for his actions. Man is held accountable against the criteria which God has determined, the norms, principles, directives, commandments found in Scripture.[9] Romans 3:19 states:

> Now we know that whatever the law says it speaks to those who are under the law, so that every mouth may be stopped, and the whole world may be held accountable to God.

I Peter 3:15 directs that one should "always be prepared to make a defense to anyone who calls you to account for the hope that is in you. . . ." The parable of the talents and the final judgment scene in Matthew 25 also emphasize accountability.

But man can only be held accountable if he is responsible and has freedom to choose. He has choice so that he may respond in worship to his Creator. Man's actions are purposive and goalistic, not causistic or deterministic. Freud would say that one's behavior is caused by the actions of his parents, especially during the first few years of life and within a sexual context. Skinner says that behavior is determined by one's environment and that it is fair game for one person to try to change the behavior of another if it is considered to be for the latter's good. It is true that parents and environment influence behavior, but to say that they cause or determine behavior is to deny that one is responsible and has freedom to choose. For if one's actions are caused by his parents or determined by his environment, then he did not choose to do the action, and he consequently cannot be held accountable for it. But actions have purpose, and they are directed toward reaching personal goals. People choose what they will do, and are, therefore, accountable for those actions. They can-

---

9. Man is responsible and accountable as an individual, but he also has communal responsibilities as a member of the body of Christ for which he is accountable (e.g., the support of Christian institutions).

not blame others. They are not victims of circumstance.

The concept of accountability is a complex one, as are most concepts dealing with the nature of the child. It is difficult to answer all questions or to cover all possible situations. The point to be made, however, is that children and young people must learn to personally accept accountability for their actions. They cannot blame others. This is fundamental if any type of meaningful behavior change is to take place. Having said that, one must also take into consideration certain factors. One is the developmental level of the child. Young children move from a stimulus-response, environmentally oriented stage through a legalistic, black-and-white-sides-to-an-issue stage to the stage of abstract thinking and seeing the big picture. It might be difficult or even impossible for children to fully understand a particular concept, depending on their developmental level. Another factor to consider is the ability of a child to act in a particular way. There may be a physical or an emotional factor to take into consideration. A five-year-old child is not an adult, does not think as an adult, and cannot perform as an adult. So accountability is a biblically acceptable concept which should be consistently applied, but, due to developmental differences, variations are probable. One should be held accountable to the degree to which he possesses both insight into the particular behavior expected of him and the ability to respond as he should.

In summary, the child is both interactive and social. One must reject the position of the behaviorist which claims that the child is passive and reacts only to his environment. If he were not to have freedom to choose, he could not be held accountable. The position of the extreme humanist must also be rejected. If the child were to be solely active, independent, and autonomous, there could be no exterior criteria placed on the child, and the result would be a lack of accountability. The biblical view of the child is that he is interactive. He can initiate and he can respond. He is responsible; he has freedom to choose; he is accountable.

### 4. The Child Has Moral Awareness

This means that he is able to place a value upon something as being good or evil, higher or lower, greater or less, with reference to norms or standards. Man is created with an ability to discern the difference between right and wrong. That is a key reason why he can be held accountable for his actions. If man had freedom to choose but no sense of right or wrong or the ability to make value judgments against a set of norms, he would flounder as a ship without a rudder. Confusion and a lack of direction would result.

The Bible illustrates that man is aware of his behavior in relation to a set of standards. Such a standard was given very early in man's history. Genesis 2:16-17 states:

> And the LORD God commanded the man saying, "You may freely eat of every tree of the garden; but of the tree of the knowledge of good and evil you shall not eat, for in the day that you eat of it you shall die."

Adam and Eve understood that they had sinned and they also experienced a sense of guilt:

> Then the eyes of both were opened and they knew that they were naked; and they sewed fig leaves together and made themselves aprons. And they heard the sound of the LORD God walking in the garden in the cool of the day, and the man and his wife hid themselves from the presence of the LORD God among the trees of the garden (Gen. 3:7-8).

The law of God, then, is used as a "plumbline" (Amos 7:7-8) against which all of man's actions are measured. This sense of morality, the recognition of right and wrong, is evident in a psalm of David:

> Wash me thoroughly from my iniquity, and cleanse me from my sin! For I know my transgressions, and my sin is ever before me. Against thee, thee only, have I sinned, And done that which is evil in thy sight, so that thou art justified in thy sentence and blameless in thy judgment (Ps. 51:2-4).

Because a person has moral awareness, he has a conscience. Jeremiah 31:33 and Hebrews 8:10 speak of God placing his law into people's minds and writing it on their hearts. Man, as opposed to all other creations of God, can know the difference between right and wrong. He is a creature with moral awareness.

## 5. The Child Is Creative

He possesses creative abilities on at least three levels. First, he can emulate or create a product similar to that which someone else has already made. He can follow directions and formulate a product of his own efforts. Mentally retarded children even have little difficulty reflecting their image-bearing characteristics at this level. A second level of creativity is found in the ability to create a "new" product, something which someone else has not created before. The "newness" of the product must bear one limitation. Since only God can create a product from absolutely nothing and since he is the Source of all reality, man actually synthesizes or creates a product from aspects or components already in existence. A third level of creativity is that of aesthetics. Genesis 2:9 tells of God creating trees that were "pleasant to the sight." God not only created an original product, but he also created a beautiful product. Man's ability to appreciate the magnificence of God's handiwork in creation is limited, but man does possess the image-bearing qualities of appreciating and creating objects of beauty. Although the Fall distorted man's perception of beauty, he can develop his innate ability to appreciate and create products of beauty, whether they be in music, movement, literature, nature, architecture, or other such fields. Man is capable of recognizing and appreciating unity and harmony of expression. He is called as an image-bearing creation to give expression to the beauty of God's holiness and holy array evident within himself and in the world.

In summary, by nature the child possesses reflective but finite characteristics. He is: a unity, rational, interactive, morally aware, and creative. Each characteristic has a bearing on biblical nurture and admonition. Each must be acknowledged and acted upon by Christian teachers as they function in relationship with their children. A biblical view of the child must acknowledge the fact that he has been created in the image of God. This has great significance as one explores the task, the functions, and the nature of an image-bearer.

### The Child Is a Sinner

Attempting to describe the direction of the heart of the child has been a problem for teachers for a long time. Is the heart of the child directed essentially toward what is bad, good, or neutral? If left totally on his own, how would the child act? The extreme humanist, A. S. Niell, viewed the child as being good and thus allowed almost total freedom in his Summerhill school. The belief of contemporary behaviorists and humanists, on the other hand, is that the child is neutral. They believe he makes his decisions based on the dictates of his environment or his situation at the time, and that intrinsic goodness or badness does not predetermine the actions of the child. The historic Christian position has been that the child's heart is inclined toward evil. This was quite evident in the Puritan schools of early America in which codes of conduct were strictly enforced.

Is the heart of the child directed toward what is good, bad, or neutral? Man is not neutral, and never was. Man, in fact, was at one time good. Genesis 1:31 records: "and God saw everything that he had made, and behold, it was very good." But, as recorded in Genesis 3, Adam and Eve sinned, and their nature became a fallen one. Scripture attests to the fact that all mankind has a sinful, totally depraved nature.

> The heart is deceitful above all things and desperately corrupt; who can understand it (Jer. 17:9)?
>
> . . . all have sinned and fall short of the glory of God (Rom. 3:23).[10]

The conclusion which must be drawn from Scripture is that man is essentially inclined toward thoughts and actions which are bad or evil.

That particular conclusion is often questioned by teachers and parents because they do not see their children act in such a "satanic" manner each day. Often, and perhaps usually, their children act in a rather responsible manner. Most teachers and parents also believe that they should let their children know that the best is expected of them. Could adults honestly do that if the direction of the hearts of their children is toward bad or evil?

There are two clarifying factors which often have either not been

---

10. Also see Psalm 51:5; 53:2-3; Romans 5:12; I John 1:8.

understood or have been forgotten by Christian adults. First, man continues, even after the Fall, to bear the nature of an image-bearer. Although man's own rebellion has redirected his heart and deeply tarnished the beauty of God's image in him, he did not suddenly become "non-man." The huge gap between man and the highest animal remains. The image may have become distorted, blurred, and misdirected because of the Fall, but children continue to bear a semblance of the image of God.

This fact has important significance for how one treats children. They are to be viewed and treated as persons who have both dignity and worth. The dignity was given by God when he chose to create man in his image and to assign him a task. That dignity remains, and, since it was not given by man, it cannot be taken away by man. Children also have worth. Christians often confuse *worth* and *worthiness*. The Bible teaches that man is unworthy, and that it is only through the grace of God that Christ offers redemption. But the act of God sending his own Son to die for mankind is the ultimate evidence that God places a great amount of worth upon each individual. Scripture speaks of this in several places:

> Are not two sparrows sold for a penny? And not one of them will fall to the ground without your Father's will. But even the hairs of your head are numbered. Fear not, therefore; you are of more value than many sparrows (Matt. 10:29-31).

> For God so loved the world that he gave his only Son, that whoever believes in him should not perish but have eternal life (John 3:16).[11]

Man can indeed walk upright with his head held high, because he is of immense dignity and worth. But his eyes must at the same time reflect a prayer upward in thanksgiving to the Source of his dignity and worth. Psalm 8:4-6, 9 says it well:

> . . . what is man that thou art mindful of him, and the son of man that thou dost care for him? Yet thou has made him little less than God, and dost crown him with glory and honor. Thou has given him dominion over the works of thy hands; thou hast put

---

11. Also see Mark 10:13-16.

all things under his feet. . . . O LORD, our LORD, how majestic is thy name in all the earth!

The second fact of which many evangelical Christians are unaware is that total depravity differs from absolute depravity. Total depravity means that each thought, word, and action of man has within it the taint of sin. Absolute depravity, however, means that each thought, word, and action of man is so absolutely corrupted that there is no redeeming feature whatsoever. Total depravity means that a foreign object or substance has been mixed in with one's actions; absolute depravity means that the foreign object or substance becomes one hundred percent of one's actions. Were the latter to be true in the world today, life would be so brutal, anarchical, and corrupt that human existence would probably be impossible. God has chosen to restrain evil within this world so that his divine purposes can be carried out. God has not withdrawn his presence from his creation. He is very present, active, and in control. This creation continues to be "our Father's world."

One result of the restraint of sin within the world is the presence of various degrees of good (Rom. 2:14-15). There is natural good, which includes such actions as eating, drinking, walking, standing, and sitting. There is also civil and moral good, which includes such activities as buying, selling, doing justice, and the exercise of some knowledge or skill which promotes one's temporal welfare. Natural, civil, and moral good are performed by people each day. They are evidence of God's restraining presence, a presence that continues to be felt. But these types of good actions are conducted only on a horizontal, man-to-man, human level. The Christian, the person redeemed through the death and resurrection of Jesus Christ, can also think, speak, and act on a vertical plane. He *alone* can perform spiritual good. Once again, it is not because of his personal merit, but purely through God's grace that this is possible. For activities to be called spiritually good, they must be presented to God the Father as perfect and God-honoring. This is humanly impossible even for the Christian, but through the intercessory prayers of God the Son, this spiritual good, performed by the redeemed individual in heartfelt thankfulness and obedience, is sanctified by the blood of Christ and is offered, perfect and acceptable, to God.

In summary, Christian teachers and parents are to view their children as being sinners, as possessing a sinful nature. But two cautions must be exercised: first, the child retains his dignity and worth as an image-bearer assigned a task by his Creator; secondly, in God's restraining presence, certain types of good can be performed by all people. Sin is being restrained by God. For these reasons all schools can be places of mutual respect and order.

## The Child Can Be a New Creature in Christ

The central theme of the Bible is love—God's love for his world as expressed in the gift of his Son, the Redeemer. Despair gives way to hope. Defeat gives way to victory. The creature can be reunited with the Creator. Life can be placed into its proper context and assume its rightful purpose. Life can take on new meaning; there is a reason for it all. The first question and answer of the Heidelberg Catechism summarizes this very beautifully:

*Question:* What is your only comfort in life and death?

*Answer:* That I, with body and soul, both in life and death, am not my own, but belong to my faithful Savior Jesus Christ, who with his precious blood has fully satisfied for all my sins, and delivered me from all the power of the devil; and so preserves me that without the will of my heavenly Father not a hair can fall from my head; yea, that all things must be subservient to my salvation, whereby by His Holy Spirit He also assures me of eternal life, and makes me heartily willing and ready, henceforth, to live unto Him.

All children are created by God. All children bear the image of God. All children are sinners. But *not* all children are new creatures in Christ. That, too, is a gift from God, but it calls for a response by the individual. It is not arbitrarily imposed on people. A personal relationship with God through faith in Jesus Christ is an integral part of justification by God and signals the beginning of the restoration of the image of God that is completed by him in heaven. The widely accepted concept of the"fatherhood of God and the brotherhood of man" has important limitations. That concept was true at one time because of the creative act of God, but the first relationship with Adam and Eve was broken because of sin. Fallen man operates solely on the horizontal plane. The renewal of the relationship with God the Father can take place only through the adoptive process of brotherhood found in Christ (Rom. 8:17; Gal. 4:1-7). Men become children of God only when they place their faith on the saving act of Jesus Christ, namely atonement through his death and eternal life through his resurrection. Various portions of Scripture sum it up well:

> For as in Adam all die, so also in Christ shall all be made alive.
> . . . Thus it is written, "the first man Adam became a living be-
> ing"; the last Adam became a life-giving spirit (I Cor. 15:22, 45).

> For by grace you have been saved through faith; and this is not
> your own doing; it is the gift of God—not because of works, lest
> any man should boast (Eph. 2:8-9).[12]

This particular portion of the book is probably the most important. For one can easily talk about discipline, behavior change, and acceptable conduct, but unless the heart of the child has been touched by the Holy Spirit, his attitude will not be acceptable to God and often will not be acceptable to teachers either. As a responsible creature endowed with freedom to choose, the child is called to live a life of worshipful interaction with his Creator, Savior, and Sanctifier. He must experience conversion. This conversion is a turning from the worship of one's self (sin) and a turning to worship of the Lord. Jeremiah asks: ". . . bring me back that I may be restored, for thou art the Lord my God" (31:18). It includes a turning away from (repentance) and a turning toward (faith). Conversion is a gift of God's grace. His Holy Spirit works within persons to redirect them toward the Truth. Conversion can take place quite suddenly as with Paul on the road to Damascus (Acts 9). It can also take place over a longer period of time in a gradual manner (II Tim. 1:5; 3:15; Isa. 49:1-6) with a culmination point reached at the "age of understanding." In both cases a public acknowledgment is called for (Rom. 10: 9-10). Conversion, for the child reared in a Christian environment, is

---

12. Also see Isaiah 43:1-3a.

often experienced as a gradual process. It is a daily responding to God; it is a gradual growth in the things of God. When a child is young, his insight is more limited (I Cor. 13:11), and his response can reflect only that degree of insight. But at a particular level or stage in his spiritual growth (Luke 2:52) he will gain the degree of insight or understanding necessary for him to make a decision and commitment of a personal nature. The age of understanding and accountability is reached when the pieces of the pattern or big picture fit together or seem to make sense. At that point he becomes fully accountable before God for the response he makes to the claims of Christ on his life. He has come to the age of understanding the truth; his responsibility, then, is to act upon that truth.

The Bible does not state when the age of understanding and accountability occurs. In fact, it differs with each child because of his own developmental patterns and type of Christian nurture he has received. But, ecclesiastically (Luke 2:41ff.), psychologically, sociologically, and physically, the age of twelve (or the range from ten to fourteen) seems to be a period of great significance for the fruition of such insight, development, and maturity. It should be remembered, however, that a child's insight develops gradually. All children have a degree of insight into the things of the Lord and thus have a corresponding degree of accountability for their personal response to the Lord.[13] Since the age of understanding and accountability is impossible to determine in a generic sense, teachers and parents are to continually, but in a natural, unoppressive manner, hold before their children and young people the promises and responsibilities of the claims of Christ on their lives.

The child can become a new creature or creation in Christ. II Corinthians 5:17 states: "Therefore, if any one is in Christ, he is a new creation, the old has passed away, behold, the new has come." As a new creature in Christ, his life reveals Christ living through him:

> I have been crucified with Christ; it is no longer I who live, but Christ who lives in me; and the life I now live in the flesh I live

---

13. The same is, in fact, true for adults as well. Romans 12:3 speaks of "each according to the measure of faith which God has assigned him," and chapter 12:6 states "in proportion to our faith."

by faith in the Son of God, who loved me and gave himself for me (Gal. 3:20).

Becoming a new creature in Christ makes a difference! In fact, it is the only act which can make a meaningful and eternal difference!

### The Child and Motivation

Why do children act the way they do? What motivates them? These are questions on which much has been written. But, in essence, there appear to be four basic motivations for behavior.

### A. Rewards

These could be external rewards such as material gain or social acceptance. Rewards could also be internal such as personal satisfaction for having taken certain actions or for having reached certain goals.

Motivation based on reward is common with young children. They are very responsive to their environment; they seek experiences which have pleasant results and avoid those which have unpleasant results. Obviously, many young people and adults also seem to operate this way, but they usually are directed more from within than young children are.

There are certain limitations to the using of rewards as motivators which the Christian teacher ought to be aware of. Reinforcement[14] can be disrespectful to the child because it tends to promote dependency. Reinforcement assumes that the child cannot and should not direct his own behavior, that he cannot make good choices once he becomes aware of norms, direction, accountability, goals, and mandates from God. Reinforcement can also be harmful, first of all, because it tends to endorse unbiblical motivations for conduct. It teaches the instant gratification philosophy of hedonism and the what's-in-it-for-me philosophy of materialism. Reinforcement can be harmful also because it seeks to limit the response of the child rather than to expand it.

---

14. Reinforcement is the practice of rewarding desired behavior so as to increase the likelihood that it will be repeated. The rewards can be material, such as food or money, or they could be more social, such as praise or a pat on the back.

It seeks to elicit only one response, a response which has been pre-determined by another person. God calls for a voluntary and personal response. Creatures who bear the image of the Creator are called to respond in a creative manner.

Despite the limitations of reinforcement, there may be instances when it can be properly used. The most obvious beneficial usage is with the mentally retarded. Positive reinforcement can help mentally retarded and autistic children expand their capabilities so that they can function as more complete beings. The same can be said for very young, preschool children, whose reasoning ability is yet limited. Reinforcement can be helpful to children if it serves to expand their ability to respond to their Creator. However, with most older, normal children, reinforcement is reductionistic, tending to limit one's response, and should not be used.

## B. Fear

Fear can also be based on external or internal factors, real or imagined. Community mores, authoritarian conformity, feelings of guilt, punishment, legalism, paranoia, and power can be reflected within this category.

## C. Benevolent Concern

Persons can genuinely be concerned for others for unselfish, purely benevolent reasons. Based on God's restraining presence, one could say that such persons are able to do civil or moral good.

The one common characteristic of the three positions listed above is the sole emphasis on the *horizontal* dimension of relationships. In other words, the motivating forces for behavior are man-centered and related only to the world in which he lives. If it is true that man is intrinsically a worshipful creature, the objects of his worship are, then, not the true God. This means that the Christian must look beyond these three positions for the one ultimate motivation for behavior. The answer is found on the *vertical* plane.

## D. Soli Deo Gloria

To God be the glory! Actions become worshipful response to a sovereign God. One acts in obedience and thankfulness. This response can be called spiritual good because they are actions of the redeemed in the Lord.

If a child is not motivated out of love for God through Christ Jesus, he must be motivated for one of the first three reasons stated. An important task for Christian teachers is to encourage and guide children toward the relationship with God which serves as the basis of motivation that is in harmony with their task, functions, and nature. But teachers cannot do it alone. The Holy Spirit must be viewed as the prime motivator within the school. He is the source of insight necessary for truth to be known. He is the source of proper desires and attitudes. He is the source of power to act on what is known to be true. Scripture speaks often of this:

> When the Spirit of truth comes, he will guide you into all truth; for he will not speak on his own authority, but whatever he hears he will speak, and he will declare to you the things that are to come. He will glorify me, for he will take what is mine and declare it to you. All that the Father has is mine; therefore I said that he will take what is mine and declare it to you (John 16: 13-15).

> But the fruit of the Spirit is love, joy, peace, patience, kindness, goodness, faithfulness, gentleness, self control; against such there is no law. And those who belong to Christ Jesus have crucified the flesh with its passions and desires. If we live by the Spirit, let us also walk by the Spirit (Gal. 5:22-25).

Prayers which ask for the activating presence of the Holy Spirit are the starting point for motivation within the classroom and school. Such prayers must be a part of the child's daily experience.

The law of love found in Mark 12:29-31, which instructs people to love God and to love their neighbor, serves as a cornerstone for motivation and conduct within the school. The law of love does not speak to behaviors per se; it speaks primarily to attitudes. The law of love is not legalistically prescriptive. It speaks about heart commitment, about love for God, and then about love for one's fellow man. When one possesses an attitude of love, the actions which are a product of such an attitude tend to take care of themselves. Although this is a very simple concept, it has exciting implications for nurture within the school. The message can be sent to children: "We are not interested primarily in the establishment of rules to shape or control your behavior. We are essentially interested in your attitudes, that they reflect the command of God to love him and to love those who are your neighbors. This, in practice, means that you are to seek to obey God first of all (John 14:21), and, secondly, you are to show concern for your neighbor" (Luke 10:25-37). If this takes place, specific rules for conduct become very secondary. But the only way a child or young person can love God and then his neighbor is by personally responding to God's love through a commitment to Jesus Christ as Savior and Lord. He is able to have a biblically acceptable attitude only through a recognition and responsive acknowledgment of God's claims on his life. Scripture mandates this form of motivation:

> But I say, walk by the Spirit, and do not gratify the desires of the flesh. For the desires of the flesh are against the Spirit, and the desires of the Spirit are against the flesh; for these are opposed to each other, to prevent you from doing what you would (Gal. 5:16-17).

> Whatever you do, in word or deed, do everything in the name of the Lord Jesus, giving thanks to God the Father through him. . . . Whatever your task, work heartily, as serving the Lord and not men . . . (Col. 3:17, 23).[15]

In summary, motivation that is biblical must take into consideration the all-pervasive religious character of children. Children are created with and for a divine purpose, that of worshiping their Creator with their entire being and with all of their actions. Christian teachers are to serve as guides for children to assist them in personally discovering this purpose for their existence.

### E. Practical Considerations

The remaining portion of this section on motivation outlines in a practical way considerations that Christian teachers ought to take within the area of motivation. Three issues are dealt with: 1) the

---

15. Also see Deuteronomy 7:6, 11; Matthew 5:16; Romans 11:36–12:2; I Corinthians 6:20; I Peter 2:9.

importance of perception on motivation; 2) the child as a being; and 3) the child as a becoming.

## 1. The Importance of Perception on Motivation

In order to help a child change his conduct it is sometimes necessary either to help him see himself differently or to help him to see his environment differently.[16] The concept of environmental perception will be explained in detail at this point, while the concept of self-perception will be dealt with under "The Child as a Being."

How does a child view the objects and people within his environment? A distinction must be made, first of all, between the physical environment of the child and the psychological environment of the child. They can be and often are the same, but they also can be different. That is the reason teachers sometimes have difficulty in determining the motivation behind a particular act. For instance, the physical environment of a young person may include a typical classroom with students, desks, a teacher, and textbooks. The psychological environment of the person may include just himself, his girlfriend and an automobile which they occupied together the evening before. Obviously, the conduct of the student will not reflect the classroom situation; his mind will be elsewhere. A younger child may be thinking about the smells coming from the school lunchroom, especially if he has had no breakfast. Or, he could be viewing the classroom as a threatening environment, especially if he does not know his memory work and is scheduled to recite next.

Briefly, then, a teacher who wishes to better understand the reason for particular actions of a child should first of all attempt to view the situation (at the moment of the action) through the eyes of the child. What makes no sense to an adult may make a great deal of sense to the particular child. Not only the physical environment must be considered, but the psychological environment must be viewed through the eyes of the child. The most effective way to do this is

---

16. The child could perceive himself and his environment quite accurately and still misbehave. For instance, the classroom may be too noisy for him to study and the environment may need a change. But accurate perception can usually be handled in a forthright manner and causes few real problems.

to listen to the child by allowing him to interpret *his* view of reality. But a child's environmental perception is only half of the picture. His self-perception also influences his conduct.

## 2. The Child as a "Being"

For the child to know who he is and be able to accept himself as he is, he must perceive that he is lovable and he is loved. The latter usually comes first; when he feels loved, he usually feels lovable. It is a part of the task of the teacher to assist the child in this self-knowledge and self-acceptance.

The self-perception (self-concept, self-image) of a child often affects the manner in which he conducts himself. The young lady who views herself as pretty and outgoing seldom has difficulty conversing with and dating boys. A child who views himself as possessing great athletic prowess usually performs well in sports. On the other hand, the child who lacks confidence in that area will usually do poorly. He will also try to avoid performing in public, whether it be gym class or on the Little League playing field, because he does not want to be viewed as being incompetent. The young man who sees himself as being "dumb" often does poorly in school because he has given up trying. The point to be made is that there is a close correspondence between one's self-perception and one's ability to reach goals successfully. Those who are afraid because of a lack of self-confidence often fail in their attempts. Those who view themselves as being capable individuals usually possess the amount of self-confidence necessary to be successful, even though their natural talent is not always a predictor of the degree of success they achieve.

How does a child develop his self-perception? What determines the degree of self-confidence a child possesses? How can feelings of personal inadequacy be avoided within children? To fully understand the answers to these questions, the terms *persons of significance* and *self-fulfilling prophecy* must be explained.

The self-perception of a child is formed greatly by how he perceives the persons of significance in his life perceiving him. That complex statement has several important parts. Persons of significance are, for the young child, most often his parents. As a child grows, the teacher often becomes a person of value. Adolescents usually view their friends as being persons of great import in their lives. Children value the interactions with and opinions of people who are important in their lives more than the opinions of those who are viewed as not being very important. These important people (as viewed by the child) have great influence on the development of the child's self-perception.

Secondly, the actual perceptions by the persons of significance are not as important as how the child perceives the views of the other. For instance, it is entirely possible that a parent may view his child as being a very capable person, but he may seldom talk about this or show it by his actions. The perception or message received by the child could easily be inaccurate. He might view himself as being incapable, while his parents view him as being quite capable, but somehow never got that message through to the child. If the words "I love you" are seldom heard by the child, and if that is coupled with a lack of outward affection in the family, it is quite possible that the child could grow up feeling unloved, and, consequently, unlovable. Some children are easier to love than others. They are attractive and possess charisma. Seldom do these children grow up feeling unloved or with feelings of inadequacy, because the important people in their lives demonstrated that they were lovable and adequate. It is the "unlovable" child for whom special efforts should be made to provide attention and demonstrations of affection. The correct message must be received by the child. Teachers and parents may feel that they love and accept their children. But both words and actions are needed to convey that love. The children must feel this love acceptance—a love acceptance which is unconditional—for it to make any difference.[17]

The term *self-fulfilling prophecy* is a vital part of this feeling of acceptance by persons of significance. A child tends to "live out" the role expectations that he perceives the important people in his life have for him. To put it more simply, children often become in reality

---

17. The love must be authentic and balanced. Children who are pampered, spoiled, and "loved" can have behavioral problems, too.

what the important people in their lives think they either ought to be or have communicated that they already are. For instance, a boy for whom a football is purchased before he is old enough to walk will probably be playing high school and college football some day. The message will be received that playing football is a desirable activity and that he should be and actually is capable (with his father's help) of being rather proficient in that sport. To put it another way, environment and culture have a great bearing on the life plans and activities of a child. They do not determine, but they certainly do influence. A child who is "put down," criticized, and called such names as "stupid," "dumb," or "ugly," will also tend to live out that role rather accurately. Many people do not discover that they are not stupid, dumb, or ugly until they reach adulthood. Then it can take years to heal the wounds caused during childhood, wounds of which the emotional scars often remain throughout one's life. The concept of self-fulfilling prophecy, then, means that children tend to become what they think the important people in their lives think they either are or ought to be.

The development of a child's self-perception is about the same for all children, whether they are in a Christian school or in a secular school. A tragedy can occur, however, when Christian teachers deny to the child, through either their words or actions, who the child is. According to the humanist, the child gains his identity either from himself or from others. The Bible states, on the other hand, that a child gains his identity from God, who created him in his image and then sent his Son, Jesus Christ, to recreate him. A child's value, dignity, or worth does not depend on his actions, his self-perception, or another person's opinion of him. The Bible states that man is "little less than God," crowned with "glory and honor" (Ps. 8:5). The fact of the matter is that, although Christian teachers and parents may explain all of this to their children, unless they validate these truths through their actions, they are living a lie. Children believe actions. A lack of confirming evidence can only cause doubt and confusion in the minds and emotions of a child. Christ speaks of a person who would offend a little child as one who would be better off with a millstone around his neck and thrown into the ocean (Mark

9:36-37, 42). Children are very important people in God's sight. Christian teachers must assist the child in knowing who he truly is.

There are several reasons why a child should gain such self-understanding and self-acceptance. First, before a child can accept and respect himself he must realize that he has been created by God in his image, and that he has dignity, and commands respect because of who he is, not because of what he does. Secondly, the better a child knows himself, the more accurately and more totally he will be able to respond to his Lord. Placing it within the school setting, the more accurate the view (which happens to be a very positive view) a child has of himself, the more ably he can respond to the Lord as a student. Studies have shown that the more positive the self-concept of the student, the better the academic performance of that student. Thirdly, the child can accept and respect others only to the degree that he can accept and respect himself. Better self-understanding can lead to better understanding of and relationship to others. Finally, emotional problems are best avoided before they begin. The most effective time to begin helping an adolescent to cope with himself and his world comes many years before age thirteen.

Who, then, is the child? What kinds of things should a child understand about himself? Some answers to this question are—the child is (a):

| | |
|---|---|
| Thinker | Physical |
| Keeper of God's creation | An individual |
| Boy or girl | Member of a community |
| Sinner (forgiven) | Emotional |
| Curious | Talented |
| Able | Similar to others |
| Citizen | Limited in some areas |
| Unique | Creator |
| Social | Very important person |
| Eternal | Lovable |

It is vital for Christian teachers to acknowledge the nature of their children, and, through words and actions, to validate these truths with their children.

There are several ways in which teachers can assist their children in viewing themselves accurately. First, children are to be treated with respect, as persons having value and dignity. They are *first* of all image-bearing *persons.* Matthew 7:12 states that "whatever you wish that men would do to you, do so to them. . . ." Children are to be treated and spoken to as courteously as one would like to be treated and spoken to.

*Second,* teachers are to acknowledge the sufficiencies of their children at least as much as they acknowledge their deficiencies. In other words, share with the child what he is doing correctly rather than what he is doing incorrectly. Be positive, not negative. "Light the candle" rather than "curse the darkness." Be a builder rather than a fixer. Help the child to build upon and expand his strengths rather than constantly point out deficiencies which need "fixing." That does not mean that limitations are to be ignored. It is just that most children are quite aware of their limitations. They do not need much help to discover them. They do need help, however, on how to cope with their limitations. They also need help to discover and uncover their abilities.

*Third,* teachers are to treat their children as being unique. Each is different and should not be dealt with in a "blueprint" or "assembly line" fashion. The "normal curve" used for grading purposes within many schools insists that some children are to fail. In contrast, Christian schools are to provide experiences for children in which they can find a measure of success. Most schools are oriented toward the academically capable. They must, rather, become places where the needs and capabilities of all children can be acknowledged. Not all children can be successful in everything. But all children can be successful in *something.* These are important challenges for the Christian teacher to consider.

*Finally,* the accurate perception of one's environment and of one's self must come together within a healthy and facilitative setting. The atmosphere of the Christian school is to reflect the love and acceptance which Jesus Christ died to bring to his people.

A teacher who creates an atmosphere in which a child feels threatened—by the teacher, other children, or such things as grades— will be less effective as a teacher than one who creates a loving and accepting atmosphere. When children feel threatened, two interesting things affect their abilities to perceive. One of these is an effect called "tunnel vision." The field of perception becomes narrowed to the point that children perceive only the persons or objects that threaten them. Obviously, a child who feels threatened will usually concentrate only on the person or object which is perceived as being threatening. Not much learning or growth can take place as a result. A second effect of threat is to force the child to defend his existing position. His mind can become closed and rigid. A new viewpoint, reasoning, or a change in position are usually unacceptable until the feeling of threat is removed.

A primary reason for feeling threatened is the fear associated with failure and its consequences. Thus, an important aspect of motivation is that of making it safe for children to risk failure. The major obstacle to learning is fear—fear of failure, fear of criticism, fear of appearing stupid. An interesting factor that is often related to the child's fear is the teacher who fears to make a mistake. Unless a teacher can tolerate making mistakes, he cannot be spontaneous, and spontaneity is a quality much needed in dealing with children who are naturally spontaneous and creative.

A teacher must be able to identify and understand the feelings that are present within the classroom. He must communicate, either verbally or non-verbally, that all feelings are legitimate. This does not mean, however, that the mode of expressing one's feelings is always legitimate. The teacher is to help the child deal with his feelings in a manner which is in harmony with biblical norms for acceptable and appropriate conduct.

Finally, the process of empathetic understanding must be authentic, or it can produce an effect opposite from the one desired. Giving love and praise to children cannot be simply a technique, a device, or a strategy. It must be genuine and sincere; it must be the real thing.

*     *     *     *     *

In summary, the child is called to acknowledge that he has value and dignity, and he is to respond accordingly. That message must be received, however, from the important people in his life. These people are to create an atmosphere within the school and home that promotes openness, acceptance, and growth. The child is a "being"; he must have self-knowledge, self-acceptance, and then act responsively.

### 3. The Child as a "Becoming"

The child is not only a "being" with dignity and worth, he is also a "becoming." Children are human "beings" and human "becomings." They have growth potential, and they have growth motivation. As one who has freedom to choose, as one who is called and able to respond, and as one with needs, interests, goals, talents, and abilities, man seeks forward motions toward actualization. Unredeemed man is self centered in this quest; redeemed man is God centered.

The child's conduct is not caused by the actions of his parents, nor are the child's actions predetermined by his environment. Also, the child was not created as one to be motivated out of fear of punishment. It is true that all these forms of motivation can influence his conduct, but since the child possesses free choice, they do not cause his behavior. He remains personally responsible and accountable for his actions.

Rather the child's conduct is understood within a forward-looking, goalistic, purposive framework. He sets goals for himself which he attempts to reach. He has direction and purpose in his conduct. He is neither a victim nor a puppet. He seeks growth, fulfillment, and actualization. That is the way he was created to be. God, at the beginning of time, gave man a creation with great potential. He did not give him one which was completely developed. He also gave man great potential. Man was meant to come together with creation to develop it. It was to be a process of growth and development (Gen. 1:28; 2:15). Man was given the task, the ability to respond and, consequently, is held accountable for the manner in which the task of growth and development is carried out (Matt. 25:14-30).

Man is meant to be a creator. Job 10:8-9 speaks of God fashioning man as clay. Man as an image-bearer seeks to emulate the supreme Potter as he responds to his environment, manipulates events and objects, and seeks to develop a level of competence with the aspects of reality that he encounters. This competence (process) motivation is an inherent part of man's very being, a characteristic given to man for the purpose of fulfilling the cultural mandate. But man also has the quality of achievement (product) motivation. In Genesis 1, God continually views the finished products of his creation and declares them to be "good." Man, too, gains a joyous sense of satisfaction and completion as he views a product created by his own hands.

Some people enjoy the creation process as much or more than the product created. Others enjoy the product more. But seldom does one enjoy a process which has no product. One needs goals, purposes, and a termination point. He needs closure. The end must be as certain as the beginning for this sense of completion to be experienced. Paul recognizes this fact as he writes in several places about process and product:

> And let us not grow weary in well-doing, for in due season we shall reap, if we do not lose heart (Gal. 6:9).

> Not that I have already obtained this or am already perfect; but I press on to make it my own, because Christ Jesus has made me his own. Brethren, I do not consider that I have made it on my own; but one thing I do, forgetting what lies behind and straining forward to what lies ahead, I press on toward the goal for the prize of the upward call of God in Christ Jesus (Phil. 3:12-14).

> I have fought the good fight, I have finished the race, I have kept the faith. Henceforth there is laid up for me the crown of righteousness, which the Lord, the righteous judge, will award to me on that Day, and not only to me but also to all who have loved his appearing (II Tim. 4:7-8).

It is true that man needs a goal toward which to strive. And there should be a time when that goal can be attained, or he will often tire and give up. But the reverse is also true. A product or goal which has been attained without allowing the person to participate in the creation process is not felt to be of as much value as one which was personally developed or created.

Competence (process) motivation and achievement (product) motivation have important implications for Christian teachers as they seek to guide children in the way that they should go. The nature of the child and the task, both given by God, must be acknowledged and acted upon.

Man is also inquisitive. Man, reflecting an omniscient God, possesses an innate desire and capacity to know. He is born with an inquisitive dimension to his nature, a desire to explore and to discover. It was upon this innate characteristic that Satan based the temptation leading to the Fall. Genesis 3:5-6 speaks of the desire to know and to be wise. Eve wanted to know, but for the wrong reason. Her seeking after knowledge was not for the purpose of subduing and having dominion for God's glory, but for the purpose of becoming as God.

Both of these characteristics of man, that of being a creator with an innate desire for competence and achievement, and that of being a knower with the desire to discover and uncover truth, serve as motivating forces which all children possess as image-bearers of God. For valid and authentic instruction and learning to take place in the school, the methods and materials of instruction are to acknowledge such factors. Biblical instruction, therefore, includes the validation of God's truth as found both in the child and in creation.

\* \* \* \* \*

The late Abraham Maslow did a great deal of work in the area of growth motivation and developed a model which can be helpful to Christians and to non-Christians alike. He has systematized his theory of motivation through a hierarchy of needs. They are:

7. Aesthetic needs
6. Desire to know and understand     (Higher Being Needs)
5. Need for self-actualization

___

4. Esteem needs
3. Love and belonging needs
2. Safety needs     (Deficiency Needs)
1. Physiological needs

According to Maslow, all persons begin with the first level, physiological needs, and then move towards the "higher-level needs" of self-actualization. One must have much of his need met at each level before he can move to the next level. The first four levels are called deficiency needs and the final three levels are called higher being needs. A person is dependent upon others to have his deficiency needs met; however, Maslow states that a person can meet his higher being needs by himself. If a child feels threatened, unloved, or worthless, he cannot reach self-actualization, according to Maslow.

Christian teachers can use certain aspects of Maslow's hierarchy of needs. It does contain a great deal of truth. Concern must be shown for the physical and safety needs of children in the same manner as Christ healed the sick and fed the hungry. Christian educators must also recognize that a child who feels threatened in a classroom, is rejected by the group, or does not like himself very much is not going to learn as easily. But the educator who seeks a scriptural view of students and reality has an advantage over the humanist. He gains insight from the Creator of those students, insight which is necessary to produce the harmony originally intended between man and the world.

The humanist sees "self-acceptance" and "membership in the group" as strong factors in motivation. So does the Christian. And the humanist sees man as self-actualizing, as a "becoming." So does the Christian. If there is such agreement, just where, then, are the differences? The unredeemed man, who ignores, rejects, or denies a personal God, is indeed motivated by such goals as self-actualization, fulfillment of needs, and belonging to the group. The source of his direction and the goal itself are self-centered. The redeemed individual looks to the Lord for his direction and as his *raison d'etre.* There is an eternal difference between the two. The question can be raised whether Maslow's hierarchy of needs is, in fact, self-realization or whether it is self-indulgence. It fails to take into consideration moral and spiritual needs. The hierarchy is self-serving in the sense that one must transcend needs for goals of service. And how can the hierarchy of needs explain Christian martyrs over the ages who were willing to sacrifice all of their "needs" for service to God and their fellowman?

It seems as though all men have a desire to be free and to be whole, that all men feel that they have a destiny beyond their present condition and accomplishments. But most people do not see this emptiness, this constant questing after fulfillment, as resulting from a separation from God. Man would rather blame his restlessness on a lack of achievement or his inability to gain control over his environment.

Only through a conversion experience can man find the freedom and the wholeness for which he quests. Only in conversion can man find actualization as he was created to find it. Redeemed and converted man lives in harmony with his Creator. He knows where he came from, who he is, why he is here, and where he is going. That, in itself, is powerful motivation.

*     *     *     *     *

In summary, biblically acceptable motivation for one's actions comes from God. The child is to perceive himself and his world in a biblically accurate manner. This truth comes only from God. The desire and power to act on this truth also comes from God, as the Holy Spirit operates within children for God's glory.

### The Child and Learning

One could, perhaps, question the rationale for including a section on learning within a book on a biblical approach to discipline. What has learning to do with discipline? For one thing, understanding the manner in which children learn and acting upon that knowledge should promote learning experiences that are personally meaningful for the child. Meaningful learning helps a child to remain busy in a constructive way; it helps to reduce the amount of misbehavior which often occurs when learning is not personally meaningful.

Another reason for including a section on learning is that instruction is a vital part of the disciplining or nurturing process. The instruction of children in the ways of the Lord can take many forms, some of which are dealt with in these pages.

If it is true that all aspects of reality are interconnected and interrelated, certainly learning has much to do with instruction, correction, and admonition. The developmental levels of a child have everything to do with motivation, which has everything to do with learning, which in turn has everything to do with motivation and conduct.

This section on learning deals with the topic in a very non-technical manner. There already are many books on the market which provide

in-depth studies of learning theory. An attempt is made here to
touch on a few topics that are probably not dealt with in such books,
topics which have a direct relationship to the matter of biblical discipline. The four topics to be explored are the following: 1) The
Nature of Biblical Knowing; 2) The Process of Biblical Knowing;
3) Implications of Man's Unity and Integration; and 4) Implications
of Man's Uniqueness.

### 1. The Nature of Biblical Knowing

The behaviorist equates learning with behavior change. If behavior changes, learning is taking place. If behavior does not change
in an observable and measurable form, learning does not take place.
This viewpoint is, of course, tied directly to the stimulus-response
theory of man. Man is viewed as a reactor, and if he responds in a
manner which has been predetermined by another, that is viewed as
learning. The weakness of this theory is that it ignores the mind,
heart, and all other inner workings of man. It is, essentially, a mindless approach to learning. That is not to deny the fact that many of
man's stimulus-response functions are quite useful. Shifting a car or
reciting one's math tables in an automatic, "unthinking" fashion are
quite acceptable actions. But the decisive issues of life are a matter
for inner man to contemplate and evaluate before acting.

The humanist, on the other hand, does emphasize the inner workings of man. Learning is viewed as a development of insights which
provide a potentiality for behavior. This could involve the development of new insights or modifying old ones. Although the
Christian can find much in common with this theory, it has one de-
cided weakness. Humanists inevitably are man-centered, and this
shows up in their theory of learning as well. It is essentially an existential theory in that it possesses no aspect of accountability to
norms, absolutes, or persons outside of oneself. This is evident in
the fact that humanists believe that no outward evidence is necessary
to demonstrate that learning has taken place. They would like to
see such evidence, but, theoretically, one could continue acting in
exactly the same manner as before learning took place and others
must accept the fact that the learning experience was valid and real.

For the humanist, then, a change of observable behavior may be evidence that learning has occurred or is occurring, but such behavior change is not the learning. A change in behavior may occur without learning taking place; and learning may occur without any observable related changes in behavior.

Biblical knowing presents a much more complete and integrated approach to learning than the position of either the behaviorist or the humanist. Genesis 4:1 records that "Adam knew Eve his wife. . . ." This *total* giving of one person to another illustrates the biblical concept of knowing. To know, biblically, means to know in a total way. It includes both the inner workings of man, and, based on heart commitment, the outward manifestation of those workings. When Adam knew his wife, he knew her in a total way. The physical aspect was deeply intertwined with the fact that Adam was both rational and emotional as well. And, most importantly, he was a totally religious being with freedom to choose. His response to his wife was one based on heart commitment. It was a free choice. He acted on what he knew to be true. That is biblical knowing.

The words *belief* and *knowledge* have much the same meaning in Scripture. There are three interrelated, interdependent aspects to biblical belief, to biblical knowing. The Hebrew verb *yadá,* "to know," signifies a unification of intellect, feeling, and action. Thus when *yadá* is used in Scripture, it carries with it the three dimensions of thinking, feeling, and doing or responding. Biblical knowing is a *total* act.

For true knowledge or belief to occur, the child must give cognitive assent—he must understand, he must feel that something is true, and he must act upon his thinking and feeling that something is true. He must validate with action the hypothesis which was based on his thinking and feeling. This amounts to a commitment of the whole person to that which is known.

All three dimensions are necessary for true learning to take place. A child may "know" his music lessons in a cognitive sense, and he may be emotionally committed to the music lessons as well, but unless he acts on the first two dimensions of learning, the learning act is truncated and incomplete. He could, theoretically, be emotionally committed and act on that commitment, but unless he cognitively "knows" what he is doing, learning still fails to take place. And, finally, the student could cognitively understand, act on that understanding, but have no emotional commitment to the entire process. That, too, is an incomplete and unacceptable form of learning. The biblical model incorporates all three dimensions—cognitive, emotional commitment, and the response which the first two dimensions call for.

The inclusion of both commitment and response is vital to a biblical theory of learning. The behaviorist's theory ignores commitment and labels automatic, rote, and habitual responses as learning. The humanists, in turn, ignore the dimension of learning which calls for a response. Learning, in their view, does not have to be evidenced by others.

Scripture is replete with directives for, and examples (Heb. 11) of being "doers of the word, and not hearers only" (James 1:22).

> Not everyone who says to me, "Lord, Lord" shall enter the kingdom of heaven, but he who does the will of my Father who is in heaven. Everyone who hears these words of mine and does them will be like a wise man. . . . And everyone who hears these words of mine and does not do them will be like a foolish man . . . (Matt. 7:21, 24, 26).

> If you love me, you will keep my commandments. If a man loves me, he will keep my word, and my Father will love him, and we will come to him and make our home with him. He who does not love me does not keep my words; and the word which you hear is not mine but the Father's who sent me (John 14:15, 23-24).

> Who is wise and understanding among you? By his good life let him show his works in the meekness of wisdom (James 3:13).

> And by this we may be sure that we know him, if we keep his commandments. He who says "I know him" but disobeys his commandments is a liar, and the truth is not in him; but whoever keeps his word, in him truly love for God is perfected (I John 2:3-5).

It is interesting to note just how integrally related are such concepts as faith-works, commitment-obedience, hearing-doing, revelation-response, knowing the truth-acting on the truth. Biblical knowing calls for man, as a responsible creature, to respond. Christ served as the perfect example through his atonement for sin, through his death on the cross. He understood what was necessary for him to do; he was committed to this act. But for mankind to live he actually had to die. He had to be a doer of the Word.

Biblical knowing has much to say to Christian teachers. As nurture or discipline is provided, the goal is to have the child know. His actions are to be based on understanding and commitment. For meaningful behavior change to take place, one must know in the biblical sense. Both instruction and correction have biblical knowing as their goal.

## 2. The Process of Biblical Knowing

Assisting children in the development of insight or understanding is a primary part of biblical nurture. But teachers are limited in their ability to assure that their children possess insight. It is the Holy Spirit working in the hearts and minds of children who provides true insight. He is the One who causes it all "to make sense." He is the necessary force for true insight to take place. He is also necessary for true commitment to take place. And he is necessary as the activating agent and power for one to respond in a true manner. The Holy Spirit is the key to true learning.

But our Father, God, has commanded parents to nurture. He operates, often, through human instruments. The task for Christian adults is to teach children so that they understand (have insight into) the things of God. That process is complicated because children are both complicated and unique. But there are certain factors which can be both understood and utilized by teachers.

Children are to know the truth. The truth of God as revealed in his Scriptures and in his creation gives evidence of certain characteristics. God's truth is wholistic—a whole, rather than simply a series of unrelated parts. Within the unity of the whole is found diversity. Each varied thread of this diversity remains, however, a vital part of the whole. Each diverse part of God's truth is interrelated to and interdependent on other parts. Each part has its own role, purpose, and function. But each part is meant to exist in harmonious relationship to each other part within the fundamental unity. No part is autonomous. Truth reflects order, patterns, and structure. These characteristics are abundantly evident within both God's special revelation, the Bible, *and* his natural revelation, the creation. The Creator is a God of order. He desires that his people reflect this attribute. I Corinthians 14:30 and 40 direct that "all things should be done decently and in order, . . . for God is not a God of confusion but of peace."

But not only are children called to know the truth, they themselves have been created by the God who is Truth. They have been created to fit naturally and meaningfully into the whole of creation. They have been given the necessary tools and abilities to function in a purposeful manner as they seek to *know* the Truth and to *act* upon the Truth.

The learning process for the child, then, reflects the characteristics of God and his truth. Learning for the child includes perceptions which form into concepts which in turn form into a conceptual structure. When that conceptual structure or framework accurately reflects reality as God has created it, insight or understanding can take place. When the pattern of God's truth is seen by the child as a meaningful whole, insight occurs. It suddenly "all makes sense."

Meaningful learning can take place only within context. The child must see the whole or context before moving to the parts. Facts by themselves are meaningless. Facts take on meaning only when they are viewed in relationship to each other and to the whole. To abstract a portion of reality for the purpose of analysis is valid only when the context and framework is dealt with first and when the piece of reality is placed back into context upon completion of the study. No two concepts are mutually exclusive; everything to some degree and in some sense is dependent upon everything else, and all aspects of reality remain a part of the context or whole.

The approach of the behaviorist runs counter to this. The behaviorist believes that the sum total of the parts equals the whole. This approach can be illustrated by the analogy of a person receiving a box containing all the parts of a bicycle and assuming that one has a bicycle even though the parts are not together. The humanist and the Christian seem to agree that one must, rather, begin with the *gestalt* (the whole) and that the whole is greater than the sum of the parts. In that case, the parts of the bicycle must be assembled together in an interdependent and interrelated "whole" before one can consider it to be a bicycle in the full sense of the term. A person must always be able to see the individual "trees" in relationship to the entire "forest."

This is an important concept to understand as one deals with differentiation, a vital part of the learning process. Children are to learn to discriminate among the various aspects or parts of reality. God has created diversity and variety within his basic unity. To better appreciate the beauty of his mosaic workmanship, and to better develop these aspects of creation, children must learn to see differences. They are to learn how to analyze and to determine how things are different from each other. It is a matter of breaking things down according to a particular plan or set of criteria. Children *must* learn to discern particulars and to see how they differ from each other.

Generalization is a second step in the learning process. Not only must children learn to discriminate—see how aspects of creation differ—but they must also learn to see the interrelationships among the aspects of creation—how they are similar. Ideas and objects can be classified according to a generic idea or concept. The pieces of reality can be categorized according to a particular pattern or structure. Children are to be taught organization by way of the generalization process. Children must be led to see God's world as a place with structure, relationships, and patterns.

A third step in the learning process is restructurization. This is the creative act of reforming the parts or aspects of creation into a new pattern or set of relationships. The cultural mandate directs man to have dominion and to subdue the earth. Man is to be a reformer and a transformer of culture for God's sake. This is done through the restructurization process. Children are to be taught how to develop their abilities as image-bearing creators. Opportunity must be provided for children to create their own products, to see interrelationships through the synthesizing of new products from other products already discovered.

Finally, there is the matter of transfer. The child through his response should be able to use the insights gained within new situations. He should be able to apply the concept learned. The goal is one of independence. To see and to use new applications for a concept which has been learned is to be exercising creative independence. Freedom to function as God intended is the result. Learning must be transferable to new and different situations so that children can cope with the various experiences of life. They must be taught to see the commonalities of life, the structure, and the interrelated patterns which have been created into reality.

### 3. Implications of Man's Unity and Integration

Children are *gestalts* of interrelated diversity. Biblical learning can take place when *all* dimensions of the child are involved in the learning process. Children are to learn in a total holistic way. This means that they must be allowed to function as persons with rational, physical, emotional, and social dimensions. Since the rational side of learning has historically been the point of focus and thus should be well understood, only the latter three aspects will be explained further.

First, the physical dimension of children must be acknowledged in the learning process. God has created children with five senses, through which they are able to perceive reality. It is both pragmatic and authentic for the children to use as many of their senses as possible in order to facilitate learning. The more avenues of communication used, the more likely the message decoded by the learner will be the same as the one originally encoded. But even beyond this pragmatism, God meant for total man to enjoy and explore total creation. To simply hear or to read about a flower without seeing, touching, and smelling a flower is not experiencing reality as God desires us to. The unity of the child finds expression in the use of all of his five senses in the learning process.

The younger the child, the more physically responsive he is to his environment. Young children must be allowed time for movement and exploration. They learn rather well through discovery at a young age. They should be allowed to experience their learning. The learning process for a young child takes place as much through his finger tips as through his head. As mentioned before, perceptions lead to concept formation, which leads to the structure of a personal conceptual framework. The physical dimension of a child is meant to facilitate this process.

The emotional dimension of children has already been alluded to in the section on biblical knowing. The feelings and attitudes of the child must be recognized and dealt with. This is vital within the area of conflict resolution as well. To ignore or deny the part emotions play within the learning process would be to deal with only a part of the child. Jesus, as a total person, demonstrated his emotions many times during his earthly ministry. John 11:35 records that "Jesus wept" over the death of his friend Lazarus. He also exhibited what is often termed "righteous indignation" as he cast the money changers out of the temple (John 2:13-17). And he was "greatly distressed and troubled" while in Gethsemane the night before his death (Mark 14:32-36). The emotional dimension of a child is both a valid and a vital part of his nature, his experience, and his learning processes.

Finally, children have a social dimension as well. Since they are interactive by nature, children can learn from others and can teach others. Vocabulary and concept development can be greatly facilitated through small group discussions. Problem-solving techniques can be learned through the committee approach. But, most important, proper interpersonal relations can be developed when there is room for personal interaction within a learning situation. Allowing *all* persons to contribute validates the "I–Thou"[18] relationship of mutual respect. Unless all contribute, the creative process and product of the entire class or school is limited. All persons *can* be important

---

18. The "I–Thou" relationship is one of mutual respect, of a subject to another subject. The other person is treated as one having dignity and worth, as one whose opinions, needs, and aspirations are as legitimate as one's own. It is not a subject to object relationship (I–It) in which one is viewed as an object to be used or manipulated.

contributors. And such open interaction between adults and children, between children and other children, provides a desirable context for the resolving of possible behavioral problems as well.

### 4. Implications of Man's Uniqueness

It has previously been stated that each child possesses dignity and worth and that each child has been created by God as a unique person for a particular purpose. If these assumptions are true, then teachers have the responsibility to validate these truths as they deal with their children. A personalized approach to education is one way to do that. It must be recognized that personalized education and individualized education are not necessarily the same. Individualized education can be best illustrated through the use of programmed instruction. The child works by himself at his own pace, but the program does not necessarily take any or all of his personal needs and goals into consideration. A personalized program, on the other hand, can include individualized work, small group activities, or large group sessions—depending on the particular child's capabilities, needs, and goals. Before lessons are prepared for a particular student, class, or school, a "needs assessment" can be conducted and a program developed which reflects the priority of needs.

This approach is similar to that of the humanist. But a biblical approach includes another dimension. A child's felt needs must not be the *sole* criteria for the "how" or "what" of that which is to be learned. A child has needs beyond his immediate experience that must also be met. These might be of a more long-range nature and most certainly must be centered around a balanced study of God's truth.

It was also stated before that man's existence is purposive and goalistic. This factor is a powerful motivating force. Certain of these purposes and goals are stated very broadly in Scripture and are meant for all persons to strive toward. These must certainly be dealt with both at school and at home. But many purposes and goals are as individual and unique as the children themselves. Teachers must assist a child in determining his talents and interests, and the purposes for which he is suited, called or directed. Children can be greatly assisted in their learning when they understand the purpose of their school work and the goals toward which they are heading. Some teachers use advance organizers at the beginning of each week, day, or class period in an attempt to assist the child in seeing the *gestalt* of the learning experience and his unique place in it. He can be shown the "why" to his learning. Students have an intrinsic desire to know "where they are and where they are going." For effective learning to take place, direction, purpose, and goals should be clearly understood by the children.

### Summary and Conclusions

An understanding of the nature of children is a necessary prerequisite to providing biblical discipline for them. Such an understanding provides the context or structure within which Christian teachers are to operate.

The child is a complex being. He is also a totally religious being, a fact which has implications for all of his relationships and actions. A child is a creation of God, an image-bearing creature who has a task, a function, and a reflective nature. But he is also a sinner, one who can gain personal meaning for life only through accepting Jesus Christ as his Savior and Lord. Motivation and learning are also vital parts of the nurturing process. They, too, gain their direction and strength through the work of the Holy Spirit.

Many behavior problems can be avoided by acting on such an understanding of the child. Such actions should begin when the child is young, not when he begins to show signs of developing a pattern of misbehavior. Dealing with the child as God has created him allows the Christian teacher to operate from insight unique to those who know the Lord.

## Chapter 2

# What Is Meant by Discipline?

Discipline is perceived as being the number one problem within the public schools of North America. Opinion polls annually verify this fact. Parents and teachers are becoming more and more concerned and upset over the seeming breakdown of order within society. Many Christian parents are opting out of the public educational system and forming Christian schools for their children for exactly that reason. Others, Christian and non-Christian alike, desire to opt out, but they cannot afford the additional tuition costs.

The sad fact is that many homes are also undergoing this same turmoil. The family, quite frankly, appears to be breaking down before our eyes. And that includes the Christian family. Some blame working mothers; others blame television; and yet others blame society as a whole. Whatever the cause, it is time for Christian professionals and parents to take hold of the situation and do something about it—beginning within their own local situation and then moving out into the community. The solution to the problem is found in one word. That word is *obedience*. God desires obedience from his people, not only because it shows that they love him, but because the directives he provides for their guidance are meant to be for their welfare. Life takes on new form, direction, and meaning when one obeys God.

The word *obedience* has two dimensions—revelation and response. One must discern or recognize the directives which God wants his people to follow. Then one must act upon those directives. This book attempts to share the message of Scripture as it speaks to the matter of nurturing children in the Lord. It is only through personal desire that one can then act on the matters shared here. A heartfelt commitment to Jesus Christ and the power of the Holy Spirit are the ingredients necessary for such action to find both temporal and eternal meaning.

The word *discipline* can mean many different things to many different people. The following is a sample of replies to the question, "When we talk about 'discipline' in the schools, just what does this mean to you?"

> Discipline is respect for the teacher on the part of the child, and respect for the child on the part of the teacher.
>
> Learning taking place without confusion.
>
> Keeping children so interested in what they are learning that obeying the rules is almost automatic.
>
> Discipline is self-control and a proper respect for other students, for those in authority.
>
> Without discipline neither school nor society can exist. The world would be bedlam.
>
> Proper discipline makes the children happier. When they run wild, they are undone by the confusion they create.

This sample shows that persons are not in agreement on the definition of the word *discipline*. There are, perhaps, three primary uses for the word within our society.

1. Discipline is something that people have. It is the degree of order which has been established in a group. Used in this noun form, it is a *thing*. Persons either possess good discipline with children, or they do not.

2. Discipline is a technique or trick which people use to establish or restore order. Used in this verb form, it is an *action* which one takes. Children are disciplined, or one disciplines children.

3. In the verb sense of the word, disciplining is often used as a euphemism for punishing.

The interesting but tragic fact is that not one of the definitions above accurately reflects the biblical definition of discipline. The Greek word used for discipline in the New Testament is *paideuō/paideia*.[1] A key verse in which this word is used is Ephesians 6:4:

---

1. The first is the verb form and the second, the noun form.

"Fathers, do not provoke your children to anger, but bring them up in the discipline and instruction of the Lord." The King James Version speaks of the *"nurture* and admonition of the Lord." This word *paideuō/paideia* can be translated as meaning either discipline or nurture, because, according to Scripture, they are one and the same.

*Paideuō/paideia* is used in various ways in the New Testament, and to better understand the meaning of discipline or nurture, we should note its two primary uses.

First, this word can refer to education in the sense of moral training:

> And Moses was instructed in all the wisdom of the Egyptians, and he was mighty in his words and deeds (Acts 7:22).

> I am a Jew, born at Tarsus in Cilicia, but brought up in this city at the feet of Gamaliel, educated according to this strict manner of the law of our fathers, being zealous for God as you all are this day (Acts 22:3).

Secondly, this word can refer to chastening or correcting:

> And the Lord's servant must not be quarrelsome but kindly to everyone, an apt teacher, forbearing, correcting his opponents with gentleness. God may perhaps grant that they will repent and come to know the truth (II Tim. 2:24-25).

> But when we are judged we are chastened by the Lord so that we may not be condemned along with the world (I Cor. 11:32).

> And have you forgotten the exhortation which addresses you as sons? "My son, do not regard lightly the discipline of the Lord, nor lose courage when you are punished by him. For the Lord disciplines him whom he loves, and chastises every son whom he receives." It is for discipline that you have to endure. God is treating you as sons; for what son is there whom his father does not discipline? If you are left without discipline, in which all have participated, then you are illegitimate children and not sons. Besides this, we have had earthly fathers to discipline us and we respected them. Shall we not much more be subject to the Father of spirits and live? For they disciplined us for a short time at their pleasure, but he disciplines us for our good, that we may share his holiness. For the moment all discipline seems painful rather than pleasant; later it yields the peaceful fruit of righteousness to those who have been trained by it (Heb. 12:5-11).

The word can also refer to whipping, but this usage is unusual.

The only time it is used in this manner in the New Testament is the time Christ was before Pilate:

> I will therefore chastise him and release him (Luke 23:16).

> A third time he said to them, "Why, what evil has he done? I have found in him no crime deserving death; I will therefore chastise him and release him" (Luke 23:22).

The closest Old Testament Hebrew equivalent to *paideuō* is *yissēr/mūsar,* which is defined to mean "admonish, correct, discipline, chastise, instruct." It generally refers to discipline in the sense of teaching or even warning a person to obey God's law, often as a corrective response to improper behavior. Two passages which reflect this are:

> Know then in your heart that, as a man disciplines his son, the LORD your God disciplines you. So you shall keep the commandments of the LORD your God, by walking in his ways and by fearing him (Deut. 8:5-6).

> Keep hold of instruction, do not let go; guard her, for she is your life. Do not enter the path of the wicked, and do not walk in the way of evil men (Prov. 4:13-14).

It is clear, then, that the biblical definition of discipline is synonymous with nurture. This discipline or nurture contains two primary emphases, that of instruction or education, and that of chastening or correcting.

Biblical discipline is based on subordination. Moses and Paul were taught by duly authorized teachers, Paul corrected his insubordinate opponents, and Pilate—as governor of Judea—whipped Jesus. But most significantly, Almighty God constantly disciplines his weak and rebellious people, who are to him as little "children." The imagery is that of immature and inexperienced children being directed toward the right goal by a more mature and experienced teacher, who stands in authority over them. As used in Scripture, this usually involves God's discipline of mere mortals or the instruction of newly won believers by more knowledgeable church leaders. But in the general realm of Christian education it also provides the most appropriate model for the teaching of younger children during their formative years.

Discipline is the responsibility of parents and teachers, a responsibility for which they themselves, because of their greater maturity, are held more accountable than the children. Adults are to take this task of discipline seriously as plans are made for the nurturing of children. This first key word in the directive found in Ephesians 6:4, discipline or nurture, consists, then, of primarily two parts: (1) instruction, education, nourishment, training; and (2) chastening and correcting.

The second part of the directive found in Ephesians 6:4 calls for instruction or admonition. This is the Greek word *noutheteō/ nouthesia*. Several other Scripture passages which use the word *noutheteō* shed light on its meaning:

> I myself am satisfied about you, my brethren, that you yourselves are full of goodness, filled with all knowledge, and able to instruct one another (Rom. 15:14).

> Now these things happened to them as a warning, but they were written down for our instruction, upon whom the end of the ages has come (I Cor. 10:11).

> Let the word of Christ dwell in you richly, teach and admonish one another in all wisdom, and sing psalms and hymns and spiritual songs with thankfulness in your hearts to God (Col. 3:16).

> But we beseech you, brethren, to respect those who labor among you and are over you in the Lord and admonish you (I Thess. 5:12).

> Do not look upon him as an enemy, but warn as a brother (II Thess. 3:15).

> As for a man who is factious, after admonishing him once or twice, have nothing more to do with him (Titus 3:10).

This word *noutheteō* seems to have several meanings different from the word *paideuō*. It seems to speak to older people rather than to children. It seems to appeal to the reasoning ability and to the understanding of the individual. It does not seek to coerce or to manipulate. It treats the counselee as a responsible and accountable person who has come to the age of reason and understanding. It is a word for biblical confrontation or counseling. Like *paideuō*, the word *noutheteō* can describe instruction which comes from above. Thus, in I Corinthians 10:11 and I Thessalonians 5:12 the believer is tutored

by God and his appointed church leaders. But *noutheteō* is not limited to that perspective, as is evident from the remaining texts. Christians are told to admonish and instruct one another in mutual sharing
of their knowledge of the faith. This word appeals more to the reasoning ability and understanding of a mature Christian, which distin-
guishes *noutheteō* from *paideuō* and reflects the different origins of the
two words. While the latter derives from *pais,* which means "child,"
the former comes from *nous,* which means "mind" or "intellect."
Accordingly, subordination gives way to coordination. We are dealing
with confrontation or counseling which treats the counselee as a
responsible person. His understanding has developed to the point of
personal accountability.

For our purposes, then, the word *paideuō/paideia,* meaning "discipline" or "nurture," seems to be more suitable for younger children.
This includes both instruction and correction. As a child becomes older
and more personally accountable for his actions, the word *noutheteō/
nouthesia,* "to admonish," becomes more applicable. The transition
will, of course, be a gradual one, occurring at various rates depending
on the persons and circumstances.

Finally, it should be remembered that instruction, correcting, and
counseling are interrelated and interdependent acts which should often
be taking place simultaneously. They are dealt with separately only
for purposes of analysis. The child is a unity and his relationship
with teachers and parents is meant to be an integral unity as well.

\* \* \* \* \*

The major aim of this book is to exegete or to determine the meaning of the word "discipline" or "nurture" and the word "admonition"
as they are found in Ephesians 6:4. Chapter 3 of this book deals with
the first aspect of biblical discipline—*instruction.* Chapter 4 explores
the other aspect of biblical discipline—*correction.* Then, chapter 5
examines the meaning and application of the word *admonition* or
*counseling.*"

## Chapter 3

# Biblical Instruction: "Preventive" Discipline

### Introduction

The first part of biblical discipline is *instruction*. This instruction is primarily the responsibility of the parents (Gen. 18:19; Eph. 6:4; I Tim. 3:4-5), but as the child's world expands beyond the home, other adults such as teachers share in that responsibility. Instruction begins when the child is born. The prayer of Samuel's mother, Hannah, reflects the attitude that Christian adults are to have toward their children: "O LORD of hosts, if thou wilt . . . not forget thy maidservant, but will give to thy maidservant a son, then I will give him to the LORD all the days of his life . . ." (I Sam. 1:11). Children are a gift from God and are to be returned to God through the process of biblical discipline. This process, which begins when the child is born, first takes the form of instruction.

Proverbs 22:6 directs Christian adults to "train up a child in the way he should go, and when he is old he will not depart from it." This verse can be paraphrased to say: "Start a child off along the proper way, and when he is old he will not turn aside from it." The analogy is that of one walking with a person along a pathway in order to give him a proper start on a journey. At some point along the way he allows the person to continue on his own, always watchful, however lest the person need further help or direction.

The Hebrew word *chanak* is used in Proverbs 22:6 and is interpreted to mean "train up a child." This same word is also used for the dedication of a house (Deut. 20:5) and of Solomon's temple (I Kings 8:63; II Chron. 7:5). The noun form of this verb is *chanukkah,* and refers to the dedication of an altar to God (Num. 7:10, 84, 88), the temple (Ps. 30), and the wall of Jerusalem (Neh.

56

12:27-30). In the last passage it is associated with purification. Thus, in the use of *chanak* in Proverbs 22:6, there are overtones of dedication and purification. Children are to be trained in the sense of dedicating them in purity to God.

The type of guidance asked of teachers and parents, then, is that of a person who has already taken a trip, who knows the pathway with its dangers *and* its pleasures. Obviously, a person who does not personally know Jesus as Savior, who has not committed his life to him as Lord, or who is not familiar with God's special revelation—the Bible—or his natural revelation—the creation—cannot lead another along pathways which have not been personally traveled.

This guidance or instruction is positive; Christian adults are to take the initiative. They are to take their children by the hand and not only lead them, but also teach them in such a way that the children can eventually navigate the pathway by themselves. The goal is self-discipline, or, if you will, Christ-discipline. Teachers and parents are to work themselves out of a job by allowing children as much freedom of choice as they can responsibly handle at each level of growth. In this manner a child can be directed to a point of dependency on Jesus Christ rather than to a dependency on others or on one's self.

Biblical instruction is not arbitrary; it is to be based on the norms found in Scripture. In II Timothy 3:14-17 Paul instructs Timothy to

> . . . continue in what you have learned and have firmly believed, knowing from whom you learned it and how from childhood you have been acquainted with the sacred writings which are able to instruct you for salvation through faith in Christ Jesus. All scripture is inspired by God and profitable for teaching, for reproof, for correction, and for training in righteousness, that the man of God may be complete, equipped for every good work.

The biblical norms for personal conduct are found in every portion of Scripture. Children are to be shown how to put on the "whole armour of God" as described in Ephesians 6:14-18:

> Stand therefore, having girded your loins with truth, and having put on the breastplate of righteousness, and having shod your feet with the equipment of the gospel of peace; besides all these, taking the shield of faith, with which you can quench all the flaming

darts of the evil one. And take the helmet of salvation, and the sword of the Spirit, which is the word of God. Pray at all times in the Spirit, with all prayer and supplication.

Children are to be instructed in such a manner that they can demonstrate the fruit of the Spirit as listed in Galatians 5:22, 23, "love, joy, peace, patience, kindness, goodness, faithfulness, gentleness, self-control." These are the goals of biblical teaching and parenting. Children are to be led into this kind of Christian maturity.

Paul's challenge of Romans 12:1, 2 must always be held before them.

> I appeal to you therefore, brethren, by the mercies of God, to present your bodies as a living sacrifice, holy and acceptable to God, which is your spiritual worship. Do not be conformed to this world but be ye transformed by the renewal of your mind, that you may prove what is the will of God, what is good and acceptable and perfect.

In summary, instruction, as the first part of biblical discipline, is primarily the responsibility of parents, but they are to receive assistance from others in the Christian community (e.g., Christian teachers). They must begin this instruction when their children are small and base it on God's Word, the Bible. The goal of such instruction is a life committed to God through Christ by the power of the Holy Spirit.

### Instruction by Word and Deed

Instruction is accomplished primarily through two means: words and actions. Both are necessary and each must be consistent with the other. How often have we heard the comment, "His actions spoke so loudly that I couldn't hear what he was saying."

Verbal instruction is commanded by God in Deuteronomy 6:4-9:

> Hear, O Israel: The LORD our God is one LORD; and you shall love the LORD your God with all your heart, and with all your soul, and with all your might. And these words which I command you this day shall be upon your heart; and you shall teach them diligently to your children, and shall talk of them when you sit in your house, and when you walk by the way, and when you lie down, and when you rise. And you shall bind them as a sign

upon your hand, and they shall be as frontlets between your eyes, and you shall write them on the doorposts of your house and on your gates.

Christian adults are to verbally instruct their children in very explicit but natural ways on who God is as revealed in his Word and creation, on the activities which God desires of his children, and on the fact that his children are to respond in loving obedience to the directives which God has given to them. This verbal interaction is to be personally meaningful to both the adult and the child. It cannot be abstract and foreign. It must be the fruit of a daily walking with God and trusting in his promises. Verbal instruction of this type is to be as natural an activity as eating and drinking. Experiences of the Christian life are to be shared by the experienced traveler with the child or young person who is just beginning that journey. Biblically accurate directions must be given, and both the "tourist traps and attractions" are to be pointed out.

All of the verbal instruction in the world is meaningless, of course, if the lifestyle of the Christian adult is not in harmony with biblical directives. The value system and the lifestyle which children eventually adopt as their own often reflect that of their parents, of whom they bore witness for many years. If there is a choice between following actions or words, actions are usually chosen because actions reveal one's *true* value system (Matt. 21:28-31a). This places a great burden of opportunity upon the Christian adult.

The greatest teaching tool adults can possess is the ability to *demonstrate* a particular concept. When children *see* how to do something and are encouraged to do it themselves, the greatest part of the teaching/learning process has taken place. Learning difficulties often occur, however, when a concept is presented in only a verbal, abstract form.

In summary, instruction is to take two forms, word and example. Christ demonstrated this as he lived and worked with his disciples. He was a visible example (Matt. 9:35); he instructed them verbally (Matt. 10; 28:19-20); he sent them out to preach and to heal. Later, he withdrew his physical presence by returning to his Father in heaven. It is this type of instruction which is a necessary part of biblical discipline. Teachers and parents are to emulate the life of Jesus Christ, and their children in turn should be able to emulate their lifestyle (I Cor. 11:1). It is this type of instruction that provides the direction and guidance necessary so that children and young people can assume personal responsibility for their actions and can avoid problem areas. This type of instruction is a form of "preventive" discipline, because it solves a great many problems before they occur. The remainder of this chapter expands on this theme, first by providing details on biblical discipline that is "caught" through informal instruction, and secondly, by describing a more formal type of instruction, biblical discipline that is "taught."

## A. Biblical Discipline That Is "Caught"

Children are always learning. Much of what they learn is unplanned or incidental learning. A great deal of this incidental learning comes through witnessing and experiencing the relationships and atmosphere within the school and home. If this is true, then such relationships and atmosphere become quite important as adults attempt to nurture or discipline their children. There are at least four elements which should be present in each classroom and home which claims the name of Christ: joy, love, respect, and security. These elements will be explained in the following manner: 1) Developing a Sense of *Joy* by Acting upon Self-Knowledge; 2) Developing Communal *Love* by Learning to Work Together; 3) Developing *Respect* by Learning to Work Separately; and 4) Developing a Sense of *Security* by Learning to Work Within Structure.

### 1. Developing a Sense of Joy by Acting upon Self-Knowledge

Children, who do not know who they are or who refuse to accept themselves as they are, often lack joy and, in fact, are usually very unhappy and unproductive people. This is not simply an unfortunate occurrence; it is wrong in God's sight. Children are to know who they are.

To restate briefly the key points of chapter 1:

Children are *created* by God, who makes no mistakes (Isa. 45:9-13).

Children are made in the very *image of God* (Gen. 1:27).

Children are *loved* by God, who sent his own Son to hold them and die for them (Mark 10:13-16; John 3:16).

Children must acknowledge who they are, but they must also respond positively to this knowledge. To reject the product of God's creative and redeeming power is to sin against God himself. Rather, children, too, must learn to accept, respect, and yes, even love themselves in the true sense of love. The failure of God's children to respond as he wishes them to respond is the fundamental cause of their academic and behavior problems.

Although each child as a responsible individual is personally accountable for his actions, his perceptions of himself are influenced to a great extent through relationships. As mentioned in chapter 1, *children usually view themselves as they think the important people in their lives view them.* If teachers, parents, and one's peer group treat a child as a lovable, talented, very important person, the child will most likely have quite a positive self-image. On the other hand, a child who is treated as one who is an unlovable, unimportant failure will most likely possess quite a negative self-image. He begins saying to himself what others have been saying to him—I am unable. Teachers have a great deal of influence on the degree of self-acceptance a child possesses. Adults do not cause self-acceptance, but they do influence.

At this point of the discussion a real danger arises. For many people the logical conclusion to draw is that teachers should simply begin treating their children as lovable, talented, and very important people. The result will be self-acceptance on the part of the child and his academic work and his conduct will improve. Well, it is not that simple. One does not treat another person kindly simply to change behavior. That is deceitful and injurious to the biblical concept of relationship. Rather, teachers are to respond positively to God's truth. That means acknowledging that each child has inherent worth and dignity as a gift from God. Children neither earn worth and dignity, nor become lovable because of what they do. They arrive in our schools already possessing these characteristices. If teachers, then, treat children in a disrespectful, unloving manner, they, by their actions, deny God's truth, and by doing so sin against God and the child.

In brief, then, adults are to treat children in a biblically acceptable manner simply because that is what God desires of them. It is true that such actions will produce good results, since God promises blessings to those who obey him and respond positively to his Word. But it is important to recognize the difference between simple obedience and behavioristic manipulation. Adults are to treat children as persons having dignity and worth, not in order to shape behavior, but as an acknowledgment of what is true. Children already possess dignity and worth; it is folly for adults to attempt to either give dignity and worth to their children or to withhold these gifts from them.

But how does one instruct children in self-knowledge, in the fact that they possess dignity and worth? Basically, the answer is the same as before—by word and by deed. The responsibility of teachers is to share a genuine warmth and acceptance with all of the children under their care. This is at best very difficult and, perhaps, humanly impossible, since there are always some children who seem to be very unlovable. But God is able to help, and he promises that his "grace is sufficient" to meet all of our needs. Christ Jesus came to earth as the perfect example of One who came to us where we were, loved us despite our unworthiness (not worthlessness), and made us new creatures, by grace and not by works. Surely, Christian teachers can try, with the help of the Holy Spirit, to practice the same selfless love with their children. Children are to be loved unconditionally.

One other means by which teachers can assist their children in self-understanding and self-acceptance is to place a greater emphasis on what they do correctly rather than on what they do incorrectly. The purpose of this is to assist children in determining the type and degree of talents God has given to them. Actually, most children are talented in all possible areas, but the level to which a particular talent can be developed differs with each child. By commenting on a performance or product, an adult can help children to differentiate and discriminate. Children can be assisted in the task of determining their areas of strengths and their areas of limitations. According to I Corinthians 12 each person is different from the next, but each has something worthwhile to contribute to the body of believers. Each person is given different abilities and each person is held accountable for what he has. Those who are faithful with the small responsibilities will be given greater ones. Scripture states:

> To one he gave five talents, to another two, to another one, to each according to his ability. . . . His master said to him, "Well done, good and faithful servant; you have been faithful over a little, I will set you over much" (Matt. 25:15, 21).

> Everyone to whom much is given, of him much will be required (Luke 12:48).

In this connection two points should be made. First, teachers can easily convey to children that they are not good enough the way they are because they could be "doing better." (Often this is a reflection of adult "ego involvement.") This drives many children to the point of giving up any effort in school because they are convinced that they have no chance to do well enough, which means: as well as others (competition); as well as they ought to do (pressure); or as well as they want to do (overambition). Teachers must have an understanding of their children and are to accept them with their particular strengths and limitations. Secondly, teachers should encourage children to choose goals which are neither too easy nor too difficult to meet. Goals which are too easily met tend to produce boredom and may result in unacceptable, attention-getting behavior. Goals which are too difficult to attain may cause such a high level of frustration that one of several negative actions may result. The student may simply give up; he may respond to his frustration by aggressive behavior; or he may take one step away from reality through the use of such defense mechanisms as rationalization, identification, or compensation. Once again, this calls for teachers and parents to assist their children in gaining self-knowledge, and then to accept themselves realistically with both their strengths and limitations.

This approach is, however, quite different from that which is normally practiced. People tend to point out deficiencies rather than to praise a job well done. This sometimes causes children to view themselves as being deficient, unable, or worthless. As has been pointed out, this is contrary to the message children should be receiving. In summary, children have strengths and limitations, as do all people. Adults are to be helpful in determining the particular talents that their children have been given, and they are to assist them in the development of those talents. Adults must also help their children to develop their less obvious talents as far as they can be developed and then to assist them in coping with the limitations which they may encounter.

Leading a child toward a clearer understanding of himself is a continuing process. It is not something that can be dealt with at a particular grade or age and then be forgotten. Children are continually moving through developmental or growth stages, which correspondingly produce changes in their self-awareness and in their self-perception. Understanding oneself while in grade one or at age six is based on a different type of insight than when one is in grade nine or at age fourteen. The typical responses to that insight will also change as children and young people mature.

There are various ways in which the topics of self-understanding and self-acceptance can be dealt with. Chapter 1 includes a list of characteristics (p. 32) which are true of all children. Such a list can be quite useful in the school. Teachers could organize special units which deal with the person of the child. They could also attempt to integrate such information within other subject areas in a more informal way. Or, focusing in on one characteristic during devotions or special "rap sessions" may seem to be the best way for some.

The topic could be introduced through the use of various questions: What does it mean to be (a) . . .? How does this make you different from other parts of creation? How does this make you similar to other parts of creation? Why is it important for you to accept yourself as this type of person? What could be the result if you were not to accept yourself as this type of person?

To summarize, perhaps the most important aspect of "preventive" or instructional discipline is assisting children to develop self-knowledge and self-acceptance. If both the knowledge and the acceptance of one's self are based on the truth and directives found in God's Word, the result will be a child or young person who possesses the joy of acknowledging who he is before God and feeling good about it.

## 2. Developing Communal Love by Learning to Work Together

Love is a word which is so misused and abused that it sometimes seems trite to speak of it today. But, returning to Scripture, one finds that God is love, and there is nothing more profound. The two great commandments call for love, apparently the basic foundational attitude for all of life's relationships. The presence of love within the school is a vital part of "preventive" or instructional discipline. As I Corinthians 13 states so beautifully, without love anything else offered to children will be empty and meaningless. The experiencing of love-in-practice is the heart and soul of biblical discipline, of biblical nurture.

Love needs a context and can best be experienced within a social setting. The school is a *very* social setting. For most children and young people the priorities found within the school setting are friends and socialization first and studies second. That is not totally bad, either. After all, the development of a child's interrelational patterns is an important part of his overall education. Perhaps schools should concentrate more on this area so that children can better learn to function within helpful and harmonious relationships.

An important goal of Christian schools is to provide children with the knowledge and the feeling that they belong to a group, that they are in proper relationship not only with God and themselves, but also with others. Relationships carry responsibilities. The faithful carrying out of these responsibilities by children is a vital part of the nurturing process.

Love can be responsibly demonstrated in many ways within the school. The concept of *acceptance* has already been mentioned within the context of self-acceptance on the part of the child. This acceptance must be extended to the acceptance of others within the community. And this must begin with the teacher showing the way.

One very important way in which an adult can demonstrate the love described in I Corinthians 13 is to accept each child as he is, unconditionally. This is one of the most difficult things for a teacher to do. Sometimes adults state that they love children when they really mean that they love certain children or children who conform to certain standards. That is not biblical love and acceptance. Biblical love was demonstrated by Jesus Christ, who came down to where man is in his sinful and unholy condition. He was called "a friend of tax collectors and sinners" (Matt. 11:19). He died for the lost. He comes to people in their unlovable condition and loves them exactly as they are. The unlovable and ill-prepared children need the time and attention of adults more than the lovable children, who usually succeed without too much special help. It is the needy child or young person to whom the message must be sent that says, "I love you, I accept you as you are; let us work together so that you may develop your potential as God intended you to."

Acceptance can be demonstrated through empathetic understanding. As Christ came to live the life of a man, so adults are to strive to attempt to understand the world of the child. The teacher must "walk within the shoes" of the child in order to view the world from a child's perspective and to understand a child's reaction to that world. Children are not miniature adults. They possess their own unique form of logic. They often think differently than adults, not because they want to, but because they are children. They act and react in a particular manner because they perceive reality in a way which is quite different from that of an adult. As one cartoonist put it, the world through the eyes of a small child often appears to be one big kneecap!

Another way to demonstrate acceptance of another person is to spend time with him. The amount of time is not as important as the quality of the experience, and, the quality is determined greatly by the lack of superficiality. It must be a *genuine* desire to communicate, to develop a relationship. And it often should take place on a one-to-one basis. The message received will be, "You care enough to take some of your precious time to notice me, to speak to me, to listen to me." The gift of time is one of the best gifts that adults can give to their children.

*Encouragement* is another expression of love. Some psychologists believe that every misbehaving child is discouraged and has chosen socially unacceptable means to find a place in the group. Whether or not this is a valid conclusion, Scripture does admonish us to "en-

courage one another and build one another up" (I Thess. 5:11).
Encouragement is best given when difficult problems are confronted.
Comfort can be given that is based on the fact that God does not allow
his children to be tempted or tried beyond what they are able to cope
with, a refining process which is meant to strengthen rather than to
destroy. Scripture states:

> Fear not, for I have redeemed you; I have called you by name,
> you are mine. When you pass through the waters I will be with
> you; and through the rivers, they shall not overwhelm you; when
> you walk through fire you shall not be burned, and the flame
> shall not consume you. For I am the LORD your God, the Holy
> One of Israel, your Savior (Isa. 43:1-3).

> No temptation has overtaken you that is not common to man.
> God is faithful, and he will not let you be tempted beyond your
> strength, but with the temptation will also provide the way of
> escape, that you may be able to endure it (I Cor. 10:13).

> In this you rejoice, though now for a little while you may have to
> suffer various trials, so that the genuineness of your faith, more
> precious than gold which though perishable is tested by fire, may
> redound to praise and glory and honor at the revelation of Jesus
> Christ (I Pet. 1:6-7).

Encouragement and praise are not necessarily synonymous. Praise
is given after some type of progress or accomplishment has taken
place. It can, indeed, be a form of encouragement. But encouragement is usually offered during a time of discouragement. It can take
*many* forms. Sometimes a physical presence is enough. At other times
a word of understanding will do. And sometimes actual assistance with
a task may be necessary. Encouragement attempts to overcome the
feeling that one is alone within an overwhelming problem or situation.
It is the sharing of one's self in a way that helps another meet his
needs of the moment.

In addition to acceptance and encouragement, love can be demonstrated by striving after a *sense of community* within the classroom.
Paul instructs us on the matter of how one should view himself in
relationship:

> Do nothing from selfishness or conceit, but in humility count
> others better than yourselves. Let each of you look not only to

his own interests, but also to the interests of others. Have this mind among yourselves, which you have in Christ Jesus, who, though he was in the form of God, did not count equality with God a thing to be grasped, but emptied himself, taking the form of a servant, being born in the likeness of men. And being found in human form he humbled himself and became obedient unto death, even death on a cross (Phil. 2:3-8).

One of the chief deterrents to the development of community is the misuse of competition. Competition per se is not condemned in Scripture, but its misuse and overuse often result in attitudes and relationships which are decidedly unbiblical. Adults often reply to a criticism of competition by citing the argument that children must be trained in competitive efforts since they will have to live in a highly competitive socety. That is a weak argument since the less competitive a person is, the better he can stand up under extreme competition. If he is merely content to do his job, then he is not disturbed by what his competitor may do or achieve. A competitive person can stand competition only if he succeeds. Competition between children by comparing their efforts or products tends to break down community and finds little sympathy with the concept of the uniqueness of the individual and the contributions each can make within a communal framework. Commendation is as justified for one's efforts and one's attitudes as it is for one's products. It is the attitude and direction of the heart which, in fact, are of ultimate concern within biblical nurture.

The sense of community, the sense of relationship within the body, can be developed within the school through joint efforts. Each member of a class must be willing to contribute toward the general welfare, which means that he must also be willing to have his personal desires overridden at times (I Cor. 13:5). He learns how to give and how to take. He also discovers that everyone cannot function as well in the same capacity as the next person (I Cor. 12:14-26). Each has his gifts and each has his limitations. He, hopefully, learns to accept himself and others within this framework. He learns how to express love within situations that are sometimes quite difficult. But that is really what love is all about (Matt. 5:43-48).

By lowering the profile of competition and promoting the concept of community, children can feel free to help those who need help. Loving one's neighbor for the child or young person can mean trying to be a friend to a very lonely child in the neighborhood or classroom. Everyone needs help at some time, and developing a sensitivity to the needs of others is an important aspect of nurturing in a biblical love. There is always a socially limited child who needs a socially adept child for a friend, a physically or athletically limited child who needs a more capable child for a partner, an academically frustrated child who needs a more able student as a tutor, a less spiritually mature child who needs a more spiritually alive child as a guide.

Within the school setting a sociogram can sometimes be used to determine which students are isolated and to locate the natural leaders. This information can be helpful in resolving certain of the social difficulties which are a normal part of any classroom. This information can also be useful if a teacher attempts to "use the group" to develop the socialization process. Children often receive useful feedback from their peers on their words, attitudes, and actions. Ideally, this is done in a loving and respectful manner. Often behavior problems are dealt with most succussfully at the peer group level. There are reasons for this. The peer group is often of more importance to the child than is the teacher. The peer group is also more often perceptive into peer behavior than is the teacher and tends to react to it in a more forthright and corrective manner. If handled properly, this type of *mutual confrontation* is a most biblical concept and should be encouraged. All corrective discipline does not have to come from the teacher. It is a communal responsibility.

In summary, love is the necessary context for the development of a Christian community within the school. Such love can be expressed through mutual acceptance, encouragement, cooperation, and correction.

### 3. Developing Respect by Learning to Work Separately

Children have a social dimension to their nature, but they are also to be viewed as individuals. Children have social responsibilities, but they also have the right to function as unique and separate people. Allowing children to be individuals requires that respect be present in relationships—respect for the individuality of others.

That type of respect is difficult for some adults to grant to their children. Children have a right to a certain latitude of respectful expression (of feelings and viewpoints) to which an adult should not feel personally threatened or involved. Squelching the right of expression simply because it may be different from one's own can produce serious tension between adults and children. Such repression can result in children expressing themselves through unacceptable actions rather than through words.

Sometimes adults see their children as an extension of themselves. Rather than viewing children as separate, unique individuals, adults can become so much a part of the lives of their children that their "ego involvement" becomes unhealthy. If a child misbehaves, it is taken as a personal disgrace. The first thought is, "What will others think of me as a teacher or parent?"

Creating an unhealthy dependence of children on adults can produce frustration. Young children are obviously very dependent on adults. But as children grow and mature they are naturally going to seek a degree of independence. They become more able to make their own decisions and perform various tasks. But if children and young people who are able to function by themselves in certain areas are not allowed to do so, but instead are forced into a continued dependence on adults, resentment can be the result. There is no blueprint which fits all situations, but the concept of unhealthy dependence is one well worth the attention of teachers as children seek a greater degree of legitimate control over their own affairs.

Children develop growth in independence through the process of responsible decision-making. This process is based on an accurate understanding and acceptance of one's self. The child must be able to say:

1. I am responsible. I have been given a task. I am both able and called to respond.

2. I have freedom to choose. My actions are not caused or predetermined for me.

3. I am accountable. I do not have license to do as I please. There are expectations placed on me, standards with which

I am to comply, and structure within which I must perform. The key word is *accountable*. There are standards. There are absolutes against which choices can and must be evaluated and there are consequences for all actions. To the extent that adults deny children the opportunity to make responsible choices and to live with the consequences, they also deny the child the opportunity to become the type of person he was created to be. Children and young people need room in which to function. They have the capability to choose. They must be allowed to exercise that capability to the degree that they can responsibly do so. There are consequences for all actions, consequences which children must "live through." They must experience them. There are standards; there is accountability. The practice of responsible decision-making will tend to counter natural attempts to create dependency and to view children as appendages of one's self.

Respect allows for diversity (Mark 9:38-40; Rom. 14:5-6; I Cor. 12:4-7). Within the Christian community especially, there seems to be a tendency to promote conformity. There is actually more room for diversity found within Scripture than many Christian groups will admit to. To deny diversity of thought and action tends to deny God's creation. Diversity, of course, has parameters which are the norms and principles found in Scripture. But the parameters are more far-reaching than often recognized. Within the Christian community, disrespect for the diversity found within the body of believers is a major problem. It is one which often causes resentment, rebellion, and behavior problems.[1]

Respect can be shown for a person's time as well. Children need *time* to be alone, to do things by themselves, to enjoy their own world. Allow them that right. Everyone does not always have to be functioning within a group structure. Children also need a *place* to be alone. Respect is to be given for privacy. They must be allowed to "get away from it all," whether it be through a book, playing in the sandbox by themselves, or being able to go to a room and close the door.

---

1. This topic is dealt with further under "Developing a Sense of Security. . . ."

Respect is shown by dealing with issues and not personalities. Ideas can be questioned without resorting to degrading the individual. Actions can be condemned without denying, in effect, the dignity of the person involved. Scripture directs that persons are to love one another even though they cannot always love or endorse the actions of the other. Too often a child is made to feel worthless, unloved, unacceptable, or rejected because of his words or actions. But worth, dignity, and respect, again, are not gifts to be given or taken by other people; they are gifts of God's grace which are given to all people, children included. Adults are to maintain a love and respect for children even though they at times must reject the words or deeds of children as being unacceptable to God and to them.

Respect can also be shown by the manner in which conflicts between adults and children are resolved. The *authoritarian* approach of adults arbitrarily deciding an issue is an example of adults winning and children losing. The *permissive* approach of adults abdicating their responsibilities and allowing children free reign is a case of children winning and adults losing. Within the framework of authority and accountability, the two parties involved, out of mutual respect and in a desire to be of biblical service to each other, are to attempt to resolve their problem, conflict, or differences in such a manner that each party can accept the solution. There is, no doubt, a point where the person in authority may have to impose a solution which seems just and equitable, but honest attempts should be made to resolve the issue through first listening to the needs and viewpoints of all parties and then to the suggestions for possible solutions. This approach rejects pure democracy because teachers and parents always stand in authority over their children; this approach, rather, promotes the concept of respect for the individual as a separate person.

Respect is shown by listening to another person. This has been alluded to, but it warrants further explanation. Most people would rather talk than listen. Most people would rather give advice than receive it. Since adults seem to do much of the official talking within classrooms and schools (a few exceptions, perhaps), the absence of a listening adult ear can become a source of tension and frustration for children. It is also pompous and disrespectful. Adults can easily give the impression that their words are more important than the words of children and young people. Jesus' disciples made that error and were rebuked by Jesus (Mark 10:13-15). Jesus took time for the children who were brought to him. If teachers could take more time to really listen to their children, they might be amazed at the information they would receive and the change which would take place in their relationships. There are reasons for this. First of all, talking to someone who is really listening can serve as a release valve for inner tensions and frustrations. Advice is sometimes unnecessary. Listening, by itself, can be helpful. Secondly, listening can help adults to understand the concerns and the problems which may be on the minds of their children. It also provides teachers and parents with the opportunity to obtain feedback on how well they are doing in the process of Christian nurture.

But there is another aspect to listening which must be emphasized. Listening involves more than just hearing the words which are being spoken; listening also involves "hearing" the feelings behind the words. Often they are more important and reveal the true message intended. Somehow adults must share the message with their children that "I hear what you are saying and I understand how you feel." This message conveys respect, concern, and serves to defuse many explosive situations.

Finally, respect must be demonstrated when a relationship is out of kilter. This could be a relationship between an adult and a child or between a child and another child. The tendency when one person is taking advantage of another is either to ignore the situation, hoping it will go away, or to over react and totally destroy what was left of the relationship. The biblical injunction is to maintain a balanced relationship with each party by demonstrating respect for the time, space, property, and person of the other. When this is out of balance, the offended party is instructed to go to the offender in love and respect and share his concerns (Matt. 18:15). This is extremely difficult and seldom happens. But that does not make it any less biblical or proper. It is the respectful way in which to keep relationships in proper balance.

To summarize, the child possesses a social dimension, but he is also an individual. Teachers are to allow him room to function as a separate individual, as one with freedom to choose, but also as one who is responsible, and as one who is personally accountable to others and to God for his choices. Children are created as persons whose uniqueness and diversity must not only be tolerated, but must be utilized for mutual edification. The individual child should be allowed to enjoy personal time and a personal place. His words or actions are not to be viewed as the source of his dignity and worth. Respect is to be shown to children and by children as they are listened to and as they seek resolutions to their problems and conflicts. Respect can be shown to children by assisting them in learning to work separately. The concept of respect for others is a vital part of "preventive" or instructional discipline. And it is more often informally "caught" than it is formally "taught."

### 4. Developing a Sense of Security by Learning to Work Within Structure

Functioning within structure is a normal condition. God has created a world that operates within certain laws or norms. The same is true of children. They have been created to function within a certain framework or structure. The strands of that structure are composed of laws, rules, or guidelines which are necessary for children to find freedom in the fullest sense of that word. This is one of the seemingly paradoxical aspects of Christian life—one must lose his life in order to save it (Matt. 16:25). Children must learn to submit to the laws of God. To attempt to function outside of that structure is to cause frustration and defeat. The analogy can be made of a train "submitting" to running on tracks so that a goal or destination can be reached as efficiently as possible. Musicians also must "submit" to the music and to the conductor for a harmonious sound to be produced. All people, no matter how great or small, exist under authority and within structure. No one, regardless of his position, can do as he pleases.

Children should have little difficulty with this concept because they often voluntarily produce their own structure within which they find freedom to operate. Each time they begin a game of some type they must first outline the rules. If there are not enough ball players to provide for a rightfielder, any player hitting a ball into rightfield is out; one can run only within the boundaries of the playground while playing tag; the first person to miss while jumping rope must take a turn at the end of the rope. Life is full of such rules, such structure, which becomes a vital part of each child's life at an early age. The simple fact of the matter is that groundrules or guidelines are necessary for people to function together as they work toward a particular goal. One must submit in order to find true freedom.

All rules or guidelines are to find their origin and expression within God's law of love: love God (obey him) and love your neighbor (have concern for him). Within this context there are certain principles to follow:

a. *Guidelines Are to Focus First of All on Attitudes and Only Secondly on Particular Behaviors*

An acceptable attitude must be the motivating force behind acceptable behavior or the behavior is deemed unacceptable in God's sight. This principle was applied at the dawn of history, when Cain and Abel offered sacrifices to God. One was acceptable, the other was unacceptable—solely because of attitude—the heart commitment (Gen. 4:3-7). God's laws of love do not deal first of all with behavior. Love is a matter of the heart. When one's heart is loving, then the actions which follow as a product of that attitude will be acceptable in God's sight (Luke 6:45). It is possible that a person could outwardly be keeping all of the Ten Commandments, but inwardly be committing murder or adultery (Matt. 23:27-28). Christ condemns this, not because of the behavior but because of an absence of heart commitment to do the will of the Father (Matt. 5:21-22, 27-28).

A key danger in attempting to change or modify the behavior of another person is to focus solely on the outward evidences of behavior. The authoritarian seeks to change behavior through power and fear; the behaviorist seeks to change behavior through manipulation and reward. Both deal only with the symptoms rather than with the causes. David, in his prayer of confession, approaches behavior change in a different manner. He acknowledges a sinful heart as being the cause and he seeks help from the only true change agent there is, God himself: "Create in me a clean heart, O God, and put a new and right spirit within me" (Ps. 51:10).

The establishment and proliferation of rules per se will solve nothing. The following of rules or guidelines without having a corresponding heart commitment is the same brand of legalism condemned by Christ throughout his earthly ministry. One must begin with providing direction for one's attitudes, the fruit of which will be acceptable behavior patterns.

### b.  Guidelines Are to Be Appropriate for the Situation

Many actions in and of themselves are neither good nor bad. Whether or not they are biblically acceptable or unacceptable depends on one's heart intent and on the situation within which they take place. Scripture states:

> I know and am persuaded in the Lord Jesus that nothing is unclean in itself, but it is unclean for any one who thinks it is unclean (Rom. 14:14).

> Eat whatever is sold in the market without raising any questions on the ground of conscience. For "the earth is the Lord's and everything in it" (I Cor. 10:25-26).

Here Paul sets forth a *principle of liberty* which states that within the laws of love one has the freedom to do what is not specifically forbidden in the Bible. But, even here, there are two secondary principles that must be taken into consideration:

### Principle of Edification or Helpfulness

I Corinthians 10:23 says that "all things are lawful, but not all things are helpful. All things are lawful, but not all things build up." Although one is free to engage in certain activities, unless he finds them to be personally helpful,[2] he should refrain.

### Principle of Love and Consideration

If your brother is being injured by what you eat, you are no

---

2. Helpful to function as an image-bearer, helpful to work at one's task, helpful to glorify God in all of life.

longer walking in love. Do not let what you eat cause the ruin of one for whom Christ died (Rom. 14:15, 19).

Only take care lest this liberty of yours somehow becomes a stumbling block to the weak. For if any one sees you, a man of knowledge, at table in an idol's temple, might he not be encouraged, if his conscience is weak, to eat food offered to idols? And so by your knowledge this weak man is destroyed, the brother for whom Christ died. Thus, sinning against your brethren and wounding their conscience when it is weak, you sin against Christ. Therefore, if food is a cause of my brother's falling, I will never eat meat, lest I cause my brother to fall (I Cor. 8:9-13).

Here, again, one is free to engage in certain activities, but if, however unintentionally, they harm or offend others, out of a love for them and for the cause of Christ he should refrain.

To summarize, rules or guidelines must reflect the great commandments of Christ to love God and love one's neighbor. These commandments deal more with attitude than with behavior. Once one's attitude is in tune with God's law of love, Scripture allows freedom of action with just two limitations—the activity should be personally helpful, and it should not be offensive or damaging to another person.

Biblical principles for conduct and relationships are to be practiced within both the school and home setting. But certain ground rules may differ between the school and home because of the nature and function of the organization. Within the school, the rules are to assist in the carrying out of the educational task. Within the home the rules are to assist in the carrying out of the family responsibilities. It is important, then, for rules to be something more than the personal whim of the teacher or the parent. They should contribute directly to the reaching of either school or family goals in a biblical, effective, and efficient manner. This item is, however, a sore spot in many classrooms and families. Too often adults impose their cultural or traditional biases on their children without relating them logically to the task to be done. Often these biases have no scriptural foundation. This type of irresponsible rulemaking is the cause for a great deal of the anger by children which Ephesians 6:4 and Colossians 3:21 warn against provoking. Ground rules, guidelines, and principles to live by must find their source in God as he has revealed himself. The rules must also fit within the nature and function of the organization for which they are intended.

Certain types of actions are neither good nor bad in themselves. A moral judgment cannot be made. They are either appropriate or inappropriate, depending on the time, place, and people involved. Rather than attempting to create rules for each time, place, and person, efforts should be made to teach children how to judge the appropriateness of their actions. Talking may be appropriate in one place, but inappropriate in another. There is nothing good or bad about talking per se. The same is true about certain other actions. Rather than labeling them morally good or bad and producing unwarranted feelings of guilt, insight into situations and criteria for evaluation should be developed.

Rules should be broad principles and they should be few in number. The summary of the law spoken by Christ is an excellent model: love God and love your neighbor. That really says it all. In addition to being broadly applicable and brief, it is also positive—another guideline. The following is an example of a set of rules which is few, broad, and positive:

1. Be wise stewards of time and property.
2. Respect the right of others:
   — to learn
   — to be free from physical harm

The first reflects love (obedience) for God, and the second reflects love (concern) for one's neighbor. There are other possibilities, but these two cover many areas of concern within the classroom and the school.

There are several biblically and educationally sound reasons for having just a few rules that are stated as broad principles. First, there are too many different situations within schools to create a rule for each one. A widely applicable principle can cover many differing circumstances. Secondly, the more rules that are incorporated, the more of a tendency there is for legalism to creep in. The *spirit* of the law is to be the guiding force rather than the *letter* of the law. Thirdly, external legalism takes away the children's freedom to choose and in turn takes away their opportunities for responsive action. The more latitude within which children can respond as unique beings, the better able they are to function as responsible image-bearers.

The question, "Who makes the rules?" is probably not as important as whether the rules are justifiable and fair in the eyes of the children. Justifiable rules are those that make sense under the circumstances. There is some "method to the madness." Rules must be fair and impartial. They should, in many instances, be applicable to the actions of *both* adults and children. Rules should be seen by children as an expression of love and concern, even though they may not always agree with them. Finally, the "game plan" should be established and thoroughly discussed *before* the "game" begins. Expectations must be public knowledge if persons are to be held accountable for their actions.

To summarize, children gain a sense of security by functioning within a framework of guidelines, a structure of rules. This is the normal situation in God's plan. Heart submission to God's laws of love is more the goal of biblical discipline than solely an authoritarian or behavioristic modifying of outward behavior. Rules should not be arbitrary; they must have purpose and reflect the institutions for which they are meant. The Bible allows a certain degree of liberty or freedom of action.

Rules are to be few, broad, and positive. They are to be justifiable and fair. They are not to be a legalistic end in themselves, but a means to an end. The Bible stands as the source of guidelines for attitudes and conduct.

## 5. Summary

Biblical instruction, the first part of biblical nurture or discipline, is received by the child as much through "incidental" teaching as through a well-planned program. The atmosphere found within a school "instructs" a child more than spoken words. The example of teachers and peer groups provides more direction and guidance than verbal mandates. The manner of living the Christian life is passed on from one generation to the next by a living example, a living testimony of the truths of Scripture and the love of God in daily action. The abstract becomes real.

The form of Christian nurture that is "caught" can be facilitated in four key ways. Children can experience *joy* through self-knowledge and self-acceptance. Children can experience communal *love* through learning to work with others. Children can experience *respect* as others allow them to function as individuals. And children can experience *security* through working within structure. Providing all of these dimensions within a school will do much toward producing a behavioral pattern that is in harmony with Scripture.

## B. Biblical Discipline That Is "Taught"

As has been pointed out, biblical discipline or nurture includes two main parts, *instruction* and *correction*. This chapter is dealing with instruction and, up to this point, has concerned itself with an informal, incidental type of instruction that is essentially "caught" by the child. Such instruction is a result of having experienced an atmosphere of Christ-honoring relationships. Christ is viewed as Redeemer, as Savior, as the only real change agent. He is also viewed as Lord of one's total person, so that one's thoughts, words, and actions come under submission to his rule. It is a very personal, experiential part of biblical discipline. And it is a very necessary part, since without heart commitment and personal lordship all other parts of discipline become empty, legalistic, and rational responses. They are meaningless in God's sight.

But there is a second type of instruction which is more of the "taught" variety. It deals with cosmic lordship more than personal lordship. It is a natural next step after heart commitment and personal lordship. After all, one is saved for a purpose—that of service. Once a person is restored into harmony with God through Jesus Christ, a logical question emerges: "Now what? Do I simply wait for the Lord's return? Or am I to be doing something?" Chapter 1 spoke to the fact that man has a task; he is to be active in God's world (II Thess. 3:6-12). The Bible serves as both a revelation of God and as a book of directives on how to live the Christian life. One such directive is the Great Commission, found in Matthew 28:

10-20, which instructs the redeemed of God to share the good news so that others may become followers of Christ. But there is a second key directive found in Scripture which answers the question: "What purpose did God have for man when he created him? What was his task to be?" Obviously, Adam and Eve, before sin entered the world, did not have to fulfill the Great Commission, since the need for a Savior was not yet evident. God *did* have a task for man, a cultural mandate, which is found in Genesis 1:28—"Be fruitful and multiply, and fill the earth and subdue it; and have dominion over the fish of the sea and over the birds of the air and over every living thing that moves upon the earth." Genesis 2:15 expands on this mandate: "The Lord God took the man and put him in the garden of Eden to till it and keep it." Several key words emerge as one formulates man's original task as given by God: subdue; dominion; till; keep. These words within their context speak of using the raw materials that God has given to man and developing them as an image-bearing creator for God's glory. Man is placed as vice-regent, caretaker, lord, and servant over creation. He is a steward who is accountable for acts of responsive stewardship.

Man after the Fall lost sight of his purpose in life and substituted man-centered exploitation of creation for the intended God-centered stewardship. Only through the reuniting of man to God, through Jesus Christ (Eph. 1:9-10), does the original mandate again take on personal meaning. Man can again seek to bring honor to God the Creator through his everyday work, through the vocation or task God has given him to work at while he is on this earth. Romans 8:18-25 speaks to these things. It is evident that creation will never be brought to a state of total honor and glory to God until Christ returns, but this fact does not dismiss man from his cultural responsibilities. Christ prayed for his kingdom to come *both* in heaven and on earth. God works through his vice-regent, redeemed man, to accomplish his divine purposes. Redeemed man becomes a citizen of God's kingdom at the moment he responds to God's call for salvation (Phil. 3:20), and that citizenship includes responsibilities to work at his task within the kingdom until the Lord returns (Matt. 24:45-46). This task includes applying such biblical concepts as truth, justice, mercy, and love to all facets of society today. This means that all occupations, all callings, all tasks take on a new, exciting, religious meaning. The once-ordinary bricklayer becomes a "cathedral builder" within an eternal kingdom. He is doing it for the glory of God (I Cor. 10:31).

If one can accept the following statments to be true, the implications for the instructional portion of nurture become obvious:

— Man is a religious being meant for eternal life.
— All of man's actions are religious responses either toward God or toward himself.
— Man's vocation or task is a part of his religious response.
— God is Creator, Sustainer, and Redeemer of the world.
— All of God's creation reflects him and is to be developed for his glory.
— All of life is religious.

If these statements are true according to Scripture, then the implications for the formal instruction of children are profound. Bible-based, Christ-centered instruction becomes the norm rather than the exception. Instruction that attempts to be neutral becomes only partial truth, which is, in essence, untruth. Christian formal instruction becomes a necessity for Christian parents, who are told to rear their children in the nurture of the Lord. It is part of their parental responsibility. Children of believing parents are to be instructed in the things of God—and God is sovereign over *all* of reality (Ps. 24; 93; 96; Isa. 45:22-23; 66:1a). Both his personal lordship and his cosmic lordship are to be acknowledged. This type of Christian formal instruction can take place *only* within a school that is committed to these biblical truths. The Christian school and the Christian teacher can be important partners in the nurturing of children in the Lord. They are to assist the Christian parent in his God given task. Each subject in the Christian school, as a reflection of created reality, takes on religious significance (Ps. 19:1; Rom. 1:20).

This, then, is instruction that must be "taught." This instruction is to be organized, planned, and executed in a more formal setting and manner. It calls for Christian parents to establish Christian schools and to work in partnership with Christian teachers so that their children can receive instruction in truth.

## 1. Teaching Authentic Content

It is one thing to talk of establishing a Christian school. It is quite another thing to do it. For a Christian school is not simply a public or private school with a religious veneer. The activities found within a Christian school are to be radically different from those in secular education. Every aspect of reality is to be viewed through the "eyeglasses" of Scripture. One's view of life and the world changes as the light of God's Word illumines from its own distinctive perspective. But, historically, not much work has been done in such areas as the development of biblically based curriculum. Curriculum development that reflects a sovereign God is often a difficult task, because most adults received their education in school systems that were based on a sacred/secular dichotomy. Such a dichotomy states that there are areas of life which are sacred (the teaching of Bible and praying) and there are areas which are secular (the teaching of history, literature, and science). Since most educators tend to teach the way they were taught, this sacred/secular dichotomy continues, even within many Christian schools. In fact, all people have a sacred/secular mind-set to some degree. Christians are constantly battling their "old nature" in an attempt to place their entire existence under the lordship of Jesus Christ. But this is the challenge which lies before Christian teachers and parents today: "What shall our children learn in a Christian school?" This question and its answer are vital to the process of biblical nurture or discipline. Teachers and parents are to share with their children *all* of the things of God. That includes *all* aspects of created reality. Colossians 1:15-20 summarizes this quite beautifully:

> He [Christ] is the image of the invisible God, the firstborn of all creation; for in him all things were created, in heaven and on earth, visible and invisible, whether thrones or dominions or principalities or authorities—all things were created through him and for him. He is before all things, and in him all things hold together. He is the head of the body, the church; he is the beginning, the firstborn from the dead, that in everything he might be pre-eminent. For in

him all the fullness of God was pleased to dwell, and through him to reconcile to himself all things, whether on earth or in heaven, making peace by the blood of the cross.

Christian parents are called to provide biblical nurture for their children. The Christian day school can be a vital part of that nurturing process. Parents are to nurture their children in the Lord because it is right. God requires that of them. It is an act of obedience.

The product of such nurture will, through God's grace, be a child who knows who he is, where he came from, why he is here, and where he is going. Both his attitude and his conduct will reflect this understanding. His education will be personally meaningful to him. And there is a reason for that. God created both man *and* the world. They were created for each other. They fit together; harmony is intended. When redeemed man views the world as God's handiwork, he is acknowledging it as his Father's world. He was created to be *in* the world and to do something *with* it for his Father's glory. When created reality is brought into the school through the curriculum and is reflected authentically (truthfully), the child should be able to find personal meaning in it. They were meant for each other. This is exactly why it is so important to have a curriculum that is *authentic,* God centered, because anything less tends to cause a sense of disharmony and a loss of personal meaning. One of the primary causes of behavior problems in schools is boredom, a lack of personal meaning. A curriculum that accurately reflects God's world is intrinsically motivating. One does not have to add gimmicks or motivational devices. They only tend to cheapen the experience. When created reality is presented *authentically,* children, created by the same God, can find personal meaning in their learning.

There are several concepts which are central to this. Briefly stated, they are as follows:

a. *Curriculum Is to Reflect the Unity Found in Christ and Within Created Reality* (Col. 1:12-20)

Creation is a unity. Each dimension is interrelated and interdependent. Most schools, however, proceed to fragmentize reality by chopping it into bits and pieces called subjects. Elementary schools are often the worst culprits, for several reasons. When a child enters school, he has a unified view of life. Yet, as he begins school, his social studies part of life is separated from his science part of life, which is separated from his language part of life. If this were not bad enough, he learns to *read* words which are not a part of his *speaking* vocabulary, he learns to *spell* other words, and learns to *define* yet another set. Interrelation and interdependence are missing. So is the type of personal meaning the child was intuitively seeking. This approach is in conflict with both his nature and with creation. Why can't one's own hearing-speaking and his reading-writing vocabulary be the same? Why can't a study of history reflect the social, geographical, economic, political, aesthetic, and musical dimensions of a particular period? For authentic teaching to take place, it must, because in reality that is the way it was. One cannot so neatly abstract for analytical study the various dimensions of life. Each dimension takes on meaning only when it is viewed in relationship and within context. Thus, the bits and pieces of reality must always be placed within the total context of reality. Anything less is fragmentation and, thus, a distortion of the truth.

b. *Curriculum Is Structured Through a Conceptual Framework*

Just as structure and norms are found within created reality, structure and norms are also to be found within the curriculum of the Christian school. The teacher is to teach conceptually. This means that principles and concepts are to provide the structure—the framework—for each lesson and for each unit of study. These principles are viewed as statements of truth which reflect reality in an authentic manner. Each of these principles or concepts is interrelated and interdependent to some degree. That is what produces harmony and personal meaning for the child. There is a pattern, there is a *gestalt* present. It makes sense to him. He is able to gain insight. In many schools, however, there is an undue concern for unrelated facts. Facts, per se, are not important within themselves, and most children realize this. Facts take on meaning when they fit within a framework of concepts, when they are viewed in relationship. The analogy of a Christmas tree can, perhaps, provide a mental picture. The branches of a Christmas tree can be viewed as being similar to the key concepts or principles found within each part of reality under study. The decorations or ornaments hanging on the branches can represent the facts—the data—which beautify, explain, and fulfil the concepts. Facts are important, but only when they find purpose within a central theme or concept.

### c. Curriculum Must Be Purposeful

The teacher and the students must know the reason why a concept or fact is important enough to teach and to learn. Children are created as purposeful beings. They set goals which they strive to attain. Unless they can see some value, some importance, to the part of reality they are studying in the classroom, it will not become a part of their personal goals and will thus lack personal meaning. The task is not quite as difficult as it first appears, however. For, if it is true that all of reality is interrelated and interdependent, there must be a built-in relationship between the study topic of the day and the life and person of the child. The relationship is there. It is up to the teacher to assist the child in uncovering it. But within many classrooms there remains a certain mindlessness. Lessons are taught because they have always been taught. There seems to be little purpose and little personal meaning. Lessons are not related to each other or to the child and his world. This fragmentation, this mindless approach to education, is another cause for many behavior problems within schools today.

To conclude this section on curriculum, it may be appropriate to quote the Statement of Purpose of a Christian college[3] which attempts to formulate its curriculum in a biblically authentic pattern:

1. to see creation as the handiwork of God and to study it with wonder and respect;

2. to acknowledge the fallen nature of ourselves and the rest of creation and to respond, in view of the renewal which begins with Christ's redemption, by seeking to bring every thought and action into obedience to Him;

---

3. Covenant College, Lookout Mountain, Tennessee.

3. to reclaim the creation for God and redirect it to the service of God and man, receiving the many valuable insights into the structure of reality provided by the good hand of God through men of learning in every age, and seeking to interpret and re-form such insights according to the Scriptures;

4. to think as Christians about culture and endeavor to make it reflect our commitment to Christ in order to glorify God and promote the true advancement of men.

## 2. Teaching in an Authoritative Manner

Instructional approaches must harmoniously reflect both the nature of the child and the nature of created reality. The "how" of education must be consistent with the "who" and "what" of education. That, of course, is the central task of the school—bringing children into meaningful contact with God's world. And it is more than simply a question of traditonal teaching versus progressive or open teaching. That is far too simplistic a way to view a very complex issue.

A teacher must first of all be able to teach authoritatively. Simply stated, he must know, from God's viewpoint, what he is doing. That presupposes the possession of a biblically correct viewpoint of—and relationship with—God, himself, his children, and the rest of creation. That is both a big order and a lifetime task. But, nonetheless, it must be strived for. It is part of the responsibility of being a Christian teacher. Here, again, there are several things a teacher should be doing:

### a. *Use Advance Organizers*

When a lesson or unit is begun, spend time presenting the context, or big picture, within which the lesson or unit is to be found. Also, attempt to show the relationship of the new lesson or unit to previously studied aspects of reality. Allow the child the opportunity to orient his thinking so that he can see where both he and previous learning fit into this new learning experience.

### b. *State Objectives*

All learning should be purposive. What type of learning should take place? What types of responses by the students are being sought?

How will one know when the objectives have been reached? What is the target? Once the teacher has arrived at suitable answers to these sometimes very difficult questions, the answers should be shared with the students, so that they know where they are going and what is expected of them when they arrive.

### c. *Present Reality Authentically*

There are, perhaps, two key ways to do this. One is to deal with created reality as it is. In educational jargon that means "using primary sources" whenever possible. To study a flower authentically, a student should have the opportunity to touch, smell, see, and perhaps even taste the flower firsthand. Learning about nature solely from a book promotes distortion. It is like gossip—the more removed information is from the original source, the more distorted it is likely to become. The use of primary sources leads naturally to the second key way to present reality in an authentic manner: learning should be experiential. Children are to be personally involved with their learning. They are to "live through" as much of their learning as possible. Although it may sound a bit trite, it is a truism nonetheless that experience is the best teacher. That is true because man has been created, not to be a passive observer, but to be an active participant within God's creation and his divine plan. If, however, children cannot actually live through an experience due to lack of time or facilities, then authentic *vicarious* experiences should be sought.

### d. *Knowledge of the Truth Calls for a Response from the Child*

True knowing in the biblical sense involves the head (rational/mind), the heart (commitment/will), and the body (action/response) as an integral whole. Children, as persons created to respond to their God within his creation, must be encouraged to *act* on the truth. Until one acts on the truth, only partial learning takes place. True knowing is incomplete. This has much to say for the type of classroom found within a Christian school. There must be room for actions and products of response, many of which should reflect the uniqueness of each child. There should be much responsible activity within each classroom; children are to be busy in response to their Lord.

Perhaps this is the proper place for an editorial note. Most Christian educators are aware of the fact that John Dewey and progressive education have been blamed for many of the ills found within North American society today. It is also true that many Christian educators have reacted to progressive education by structuring their classrooms and schools in what is often called a traditional pattern. The logical conclusion one can draw is that teaching traditionally is teaching biblically and teaching progressively or openly is teaching unbiblically. As was mentioned before, this is too simplistic an answer. *The Christian educator is called to be a responsible professional who has personally thought through an educational philosophy and psychology that reflects the child and the world as God has created both.* This foundation is then carried forward and reflected in the everyday classroom educational activities called curriculum and instruction. The final product will probably include a degree of obvious structure as well as a degree of openness. All of these must also be tempered to fit the readiness of the teacher and students, their needs, and their personalities. In summary, instructional approaches are not evil or good within themselves. Many other variables must be taken into consideration. Rigid conformity to certain instructional approaches, whatever they may be, is both a mindless and irresponsible denial of the nature, function, and purpose of man and of the world in which he is placed.

Teachers function authoritatively, then, when they know and respond to the truth as God has revealed it. They are to seek the same "revelation-response" type of experience for their children. There should not be an emphasis on one particular approach; there can be, rather, a blending of various approaches. The teacher, serving as a guide, is to direct the students to the absolutes, norms, and truths previously uncovered within God's Word and world. This should be done in the most authentic manner possible. The use of primary sources and allowing children to actually experience reality are the most honest ways of dealing with truth. Allowing children to utilize all five senses assists this honest interpretation of reality. But it remains the teacher's responsibility, within the calling and authority that he has been given under God, to lead and to guide children in a particular direction, always within a biblical, Christ-honoring context.

Such guidance should not, however, violate the child's personhood. The *I–Thou* relationship must remain. The children must be allowed to learn in a manner that is in harmony with their nature.

## C. Summary

The "preventive" or instructional portion of biblical discipline has a formal dimension as well. It is to be "taught." Adults within the Christian community are to formally instruct their children in the things of the Lord. That includes more than moral training. It includes preparing children to carry out the task that God has given them. They are to learn how to serve others and how to develop the creation for God's glory and man's enjoyment. This can best be done within a school that places Jesus Christ at its center.

The curriculum within such a school is to be *authentic,* reflecting the truth of God. It is to reflect the unity which Christ brings to created reality. It is to reflect the structure of all knowledge. This can be done by teaching interrelated concepts. The curriculum must always be personally meaningful to the child. It is to relate to his purpose for existence and to his nature.

The instructional approaches are to be *authoritative.* They must harmoniously reflect both the nature of the child and the nature of created reality.

*   *   *   *   *

Before concluding this chapter on instruction, and especially this section on curriculum and instructional approaches within the classroom, it may be profitable to share a few findings from educational research on ways to more ably maintain appropriate classroom behavior. They seem to fit rather well within the framework that has been developed so far, including such concepts as those of unity, interrelatedness, authoritativeness, and respect.

There are several characteristics and activities of teachers which tend to create a more productive atmosphere and also tend to reduce the amount of irresponsible behavior present. Most of these are of a non-verbal nature and would not normally be called teaching methods. They seem, rather, to be more a part of the teacher's person than the methods used.

1. *With-it-ness*—The teacher communicates to his children that he knows what is going on within the classroom. This is done nonverbally, by his actions rather than by his words. He seems to have "eyes in the back of his head." He is aware. He is "with it."

2. *Overlapping*—The teacher is able to handle more than one situation at a time. He does not become so immersed in one issue or one child that he loses contact with the other activities or children in the classroom.

3. *Movement management*—The teacher is able to begin, maintain, and end lessons in a manner that is smooth and has momentum. The opposite would be "jerkiness" or "slowdowns." These two terms are explained further so that the concept of movement management within the classroom can be more clearly understood.

### Jerkiness:

(a) *Goal-directedness* may be contrasted with stimulus-boundness. A teacher who is goal-directed always knows where he is heading and keeps the classroom activity moving in that particular direction. A teacher who is stimulus-bound seems to have little self-will and reacts to unplanned and irrelevant events within the classroom.

(b) A *thrust* is a teacher's sudden "busting in" or interruption of the children's activities with an order, statement, or question in a selfishly spontaneous manner. In other words, the message was not worth the disruption in learning which it caused.

(c) A *dangle* is an activity begun by a teacher and then left "hanging in midair" by going off to some other activity. Later, the activity is resumed. In *truncation,* the activity is not resumed.

(d) In a *flip-flop* the teacher terminates one activity, begins another, and then returns to the terminated activity.

### Slowdowns:

(a) *Overdwelling* occurs when a teacher dwells on an issue or activity beyond what is necessary for understanding to take place. Overdwelling would produce a reaction on the part of most children of "All right, all right, that's enough already!" There are various kinds: nagging over behavior patterns; overinstructing on where to sit, how to stand, how to hold a pencil; overemphasizing materials so that the focus of the activity is lost.

(b) *Fragmentations* are slowdowns produced by a teacher's breaking an activity down into sub-parts when the activity could be performed as a single unit.

— Group fragmentation occurs when a teacher has members of a group do singly and separately what a whole group could be doing as a unit at one time. This tends to produce waiting periods for individuals and thus slow down the movement.

— Activity fragmentation occurs when a teacher fragments a meaningful activity into smaller components and focuses upon these separate sub-parts when the activity could have been performed as a single, uninterrupted sequence.

### Summary and Conclusions

Biblical nurture or discipline begins with instruction on the things of God. This instruction is both informal and formal. Much of the instruction a child receives is of the incidental variety. He just "picks it up" by observing those people and activities around him. But biblical instruction must also be of a more formal, well-planned variety. This type of Christian education is to be found in the Christian home, the Christian church, and the Christian school, each standing in support of the others (Eccles. 4:12). This type of instruction, which calls for a heart commitment and an active response on the part of the child, does more than anything else to produce a school and home environment that is free from unacceptable and inappropriate behavior. Children must know what is expected of them; only then can they be held accountable for their actions.

## Chapter 4

# Biblical Chastening: "Corrective" Discipline

Biblical nurture or discipline has two parts—*instruction* and *correction*. Chapter 3 dealt with the matter of instruction, and now chapter 4 deals with the matter of correction. *Both* instruction and correction are necessary, and it must be pointed out that the successful implementation of the directives contained in this chapter will depend greatly on how well the instructional directives have been, are, and will continue to be carried out.

The first section of this chapter lays some necessary groundwork for biblical correction by explaining the concept of *authority*. This touches on the source, nature, and purpose of authority. The concept of chastening or correction follows, and guidelines are provided on how to handle unacceptable and inappropriate behavior. The matters of correction versus punishment and of corporal punishment per se are then dealt with.

## Authority

### A. The Source of Authority

Romans 13:1, 2 states quite explicitly that God is the source of all authority:

> Let every person be subject to the governing authorities. For there is no authority except from God, and those that exist have been instituted by God. Therefore he who resists the authorities resists what God has appointed, and those who resist will incur judgment.

In John 19:11 the same Greek word used for *authority* in Romans 13 is translated as *power*—

> Jesus answered him, "You would have no power over me unless it had been given you from above. . . ."

Both the right to act and the ability to act are gifts from God; they are a part of God's sovereign grace which he chooses to bestow on man. Teachers and parents have no intrinsic or inherent authority; all authority is delegated by God.

Authority is sometimes delegated directly from God. One example is his granting to parents specific authority over their own children (Eph. 6:1-4; Col. 3:20). This includes the authority to nurture them in the Lord. Another example is God's granting of general authority to those whom he calls to special tasks or offices within the Christian community—such as preaching or teaching (Rom. 12:6; I Cor. 12: 29; I Tim. 2:12).

Authority is often delegated indirectly from God—through another person. In Israel one of the duties of the kingly office was to teach all of God's people the ways of the Lord. But the king could delegate that authority to others (II Chron. 17:7-9). The same is true of Jesus. Although he shares the divinity of the Father, while on earth he also presented himself as a man who was sent from God (John 5:30). But he could also delegate this God-given authority to others (Luke 9:1-2; John 13:20). Part of the authority of teachers within the Christian school is of this secondary or re-delegated type. Parents have delegated to them a certain amount of their own authority to teach their children. Consequently, the teachers receive authority over the children via two routes—direct and indirect—the source of both being God.

This authority which comes from God requires, however, a response or validation on the part of teachers and parents for it to function as intended. This validating is similar to that required for the development of one's positive self-image—man's actions are to validate the fact that a person's identity comes from God. Man's actions are also to validate the fact that a person's authority comes from God. He is to respond in a manner which authentically or accurately reflects what God has already determined.

Man's response to the authority given to him is to be authoritative. Responding or acting authoritatively takes place when one knows and does the truth. Teachers are to become fully qualified professional educators, but always within a biblical framework.[1] In the case of parents, they are to seek to become knowledgeable parents by whatever means are available to them, but always within the guidelines found in Scripture. Simply stated, people in authority must know what they are doing within their particular calling. They are to speak and act authoritatively.

Man, then, is to act upon delegated authority in a responsible manner. He must: understand the nature of his task; equip himself to fulfil the task; and exercise his authority through service, seeking the welfare of others. This insight, capability, and response, too, is a gift from God. Such knowledge, expertise, and service is to be placed within a religious context if it is to be found pleasing to God. It is to be subject to the norms and directives of Scripture. This religious framework also originates with God. *All* of man's ability to exercise authority in a responsible manner originates with the sovereign God. The Holy Spirit provides the insight, desire, and power to say and to do the will of God. When this takes place, man speaks authoritatively, as one having authority.

Jesus stands out as the supreme example of one who speaks authoritatively. He recognized the source of his authority and he spoke in a truthful manner.

> And they were astonished at his teaching, for he taught them as one who had authority, and not as the scribes (Mark 1:22).

> Teacher, we know that you are true, and care for no man; for you do not regard the position of men, but truly teach the way of God . . . (Mark 12:14).

> I can do nothing on my own authority; as I hear, I judge; and my judgment is just, because I seek not my own will but the will of him who sent me (John 5:30).

These passages point out the difference between acting in an authoritarian manner and acting in an authoritative manner. Christ taught authoritatively because he knew what he was saying, he knew the Truth (John 1:17-18). He had perfect knowledge, not only of

---

1. Christian schools should seek to employ only such fully qualified professional educators as teachers, persons who are spiritually, academically, and professionally prepared.

the world around himself, but also of the relationship of that world to God. A teacher who is authoritative knows his subject area, children, how to teach, and how all of that relates to the sovereign God. He is one who "knows" in the biblical sense. He has head knowledge, heart commitment, and acts upon it. He responds with the acknowledgment that "in thy light do we see light" (Ps. 36:9). The authoritarian, on the other hand, bases his authority on sheer power. He is forced to compensate because he does not have the insight required for him to fulfil the task assigned to him. He neither validates nor authentically reflects the authority given to him by God, and his presence in the classroom tends to foster meaninglessness and disharmony.

In summary, authority comes from God. Man's task is to respond to the authority found in and of God. He can validate this authority through his actions as a teacher. His words and actions are perceived as being authoritative to the degree that he finds his insight from God's Word. To the degree that teachers are "qualified" for their positions, in the total biblical sense of being qualified, they will experience effectiveness in working with their children. The discipline and admonition must be "of the Lord," not of man. *Authority is to be carried out authoritatively*.

## B. The Nature of Authority

The nature of authority is based on two seemingly paradoxical concepts which stand in tension with each other in fashion similar to the beams of a roof structure. The two concepts are *dominion* and *service*. For authority to remain balanced, neither must predominate. They must remain in "tension." Genesis 1:28 speaks of man as having dominion over the animals, plants, and resources placed in creation. This dominion, translated for today's teachers, means that those in authority are in charge, they are responsible for what is going on. This means that they take the initiative; they give leadership and guidance; they are direction-givers. That is exactly the reason they must know what they are doing. Much is expected of them. They are in dominion as responsible and authoritative guides.

But authority has a second, often overlooked, dimension, that of service. Genesis 2:15 states that "the Lord God took the man and put him in the garden of Eden to till it and keep it." The Hebrew verb translated "till" is *'abad,* which basically means "to work" (i.e., to work the soil as to till or plow it). The verb also may mean "to serve," and this is carried forward in the cognate noun, *'ebed,* which means "slave" or "servant." Adam was given the responsibility of rendering a service in maintaining the garden of Eden. That is, his very dominion over it required him "to serve" as a common peasant in maintaining it. Teachers are to "serve" children in the sense that the welfare of the children is the goal. Adults in authority are to be helpers, helping children to develop the potential which God has given to them for his glory.

Christ emphasized the concept of *service by the one having authority,* that of all authority being given for the sake of service to (helping) others, never for the sake of personal prestige.

> And he sat down and called the twelve; and he said to them, "If any one would be first, he must be last of all and servant of all" (Mark 9:35).

> And Jesus called them to him and said to them, "You know that those who are supposed to rule over the Gentiles lord it over them, and their great men exercise authority over them. But it shall not be so among you; but whoever would be great among you must be your servant, and whoever would be first among you must be slave of all. For the Son of man also came not to be served but to serve, and to give his life as a ransom for many" (Mark 10:42-45).

> When he had washed their feet, and taken his garments and resumed his place, he said to them, "Do you know what I have done to you? You call me Teacher and Lord; and you are right, for so I am. If I then, your Lord and Teacher, have washed your feet you also ought to wash one another's feet. For I have given you an example, that you also should do as I have done to you. Truly, truly, I say to you, a servant is not greater than his master—nor is he who is sent greater than he who sent him. If you know these things, blessed are you if you do them (John 13:12-17).

Man was given both a task and the authority to perform that task. That authority calls for the exercise of both dominion and service.

The authority one person has over another is to be used for the sake of the other. When either dominion or service is missing, authority is being misused. Dominion by itself is selfish and dictatorial. Service without dominion fails to provide the leadership and direction God requires of those placed in authority. Both dominion and service must be kept in proper balance and tension.

## C. The Purpose of Authority

There are several purposes for human authority. First, society must have structure for it to function properly. A society without structure becomes anarchy and chaos. Secondly, God has a divine purpose for mankind and the world. He is directing events toward a termination point. Authority and structure are instruments used by God for the furthering of his sovereign purposes. Thirdly, the proper use of human authority can serve as an instructional model for God's authority. Children can be taught that willing submission to human authority is both a reflection and a part of a proper Creator-creature relationship with God. One who learns to submit to earthly authority finds submission to divine authority more comprehensible and meaningful. Children are told in Ephesians 6:1 to "obey [their] parents in the Lord, for this is right." The relationship of parents to their children should be a picture of the heavenly Father's relationship to his children.

\*     \*     \*     \*     \*

If authority is to portray the relationship of God to man, and if authority is meant to assist in the development of respectful and meaningful human relationships, the concepts of *freedom* and *obedience* must be explained.

### 1. Freedom

Freedom does not allow one to do as he pleases. That would be *license,* which can lead only to anarchy. Freedom comes only through submission. One can gain and maintain freedom of expression by submitting his will and actions to certain norms which have been designed to allow for such expression. The world is full of examples of freedom being gained through following a set of rules or guidelines. The heart of biblical self-discipline is the acknowledgment that ". . . you are not your own . . . for you are bought with a price . . ." (I Cor. 6:19-20). I Peter 2:9 picks up on this theme by instructing that "you are a chosen race, a royal priesthood, a holy nation, God's own people, that you may declare the wonderful deeds of him who called you out of darkness into his marvelous light." Verse 16 follows with "Live as free men, yet without using your freedom as a pretext for evil; but live as servants of God." Freedom for the Christian is found in service to God. This seemingly paradoxical situation is explained in Romans 8:2: "For the law of the Spirit of life in Christ Jesus has set me free from the law of sin and death." Freedom has been gained *from* the bondage of sin and death *to* the reality of the spirit-filled life (Rom. 6:17-18). A "broken and contrite heart" is one which finds harmony of purpose with God, self, others, and created reality. That is the way it was intended to be.

Freedom is, however, much like a river that runs between two banks. One bank is license and anarchy; the other bank is legalism and externalism. One must always function *between* these two extremes in order to remain free. Desiring license is giving in to hedonistic impulses. Desiring the security of legalism, having it all spelled out, is slavery of the opposite type. Conforming to the laws, mores, and expectations of men causes the abdication of one's responsibilities and the loss of one's freedom (Mark 2:23–3:5; 7:1-13). Both license and legalism are equally as damaging.

God gives laws to obey and directions to follow, but he does not coerce or manipulate man into obedience. He allows man the choice to obey or to disobey. But man must also bear the consequences of his decisions. Adam and Eve in the garden of Eden are the prime examples of this. And even in man's choice to obey, God allows freedom for *varied* responses within this obedience. Teachers should do no less. They should not demand blind obedience in an authoritarian manner or manipulate a response in a behavioristic manner. Such actions tend to form the children in the image of the teacher instead of allowing them to develop as image-bearers of God. Rather, teachers are to direct and guide. The *I–Thou* relationship of respect for the needs and dignity of each other must be maintained.

## 2. Obedience

Closely related to the concept of freedom is the concept of obedience. A child's response to the authority placed over him, whether it be within the school or the home, is to honor and to obey. There are many references in Scripture which indicate this. The fifth commandment, in Exodus 20:12, states: "Honor your father and your mother, that your days may be long in the land which the LORD your God gives you." The Hebrew word for honor, *kabēd/kabōd,* means "to make heavy or weighty," or in the figurative sense of considering something or someone to be important. Other verses in the Old Testament which use this word and help to explain its meaning are the following:

> . . . The LORD declares: "Far be it from me, for those who honor me I will honor, and those who despise me shall be lightly esteemed (I Sam. 2:30).

> I give you also what you have not asked, both riches and honor, so that no other king shall compare with you, all your days (I Kings 3:13).

> Honor the LORD with your substance and with the first fruits of all your produce; then your barns will be filled with plenty, and your vats will be bursting with wine (Prov. 3:9, 10).

> A son honors his father, and a servant his master. If then I am a father, where is my honor. And if I am a master, where is my fear? says the LORD of hosts to you . . . (Mal. 1:6).

The New Testament also instructs children to honor. Christ reaffirms this commandment in Matthew 19:10 by telling the rich young ruler to honor his father and mother. The Greek word for honor, *timaō/ time,* is also used within various contexts in the New Testament:

> Love one another with brotherly affection; outdo one another in showing honor (Rom. 12:10).

> Honor your father and mother (this is the first commandment with a promise) that it may be well with you and that you may live long on the earth (Eph. 6:2, 3).

> Let the elders who rule well be considered worthy of double honor, especially those who labor in preaching and teaching (I Tim. 5:17).

> Honor all men. Love the brotherhood. Fear God. Honor the emperor (I Peter 2:17).

Honor, as used in these passages, seems to indicate a sense of deference, recognition, reverence, and respect, mingled with love. Children are to honor their parents and others in authority who serve in the place of their parents.

But even more directive is the Greek word for obey, *hypakouō*. Children are told to obey their parents in Colossians 3:20: "Children, obey your parents in everything, for this pleases the Lord": and in Ephesians 6:1: "Children, obey your parents in the Lord, for this is right." The word *hypakouō* derives from *akouō*, which means to "hear" or "listen"; with the prefix *hypo* it intensifies into "listening" in the sense of "obeying." Children are to listen and to submit. Other verses in the New Testament which use this word provide amplification:

> And they were all amazed, so that they questioned among themselves, saying, "What is this? A new teaching! With authority he commands even the unclean spirits, and they obey him." (Mark 1:27).

> And they were filled with awe, and said to one another, "Who then is this, that even the wind and sea obey him?" (Mark 4:41).

> By faith Abraham obeyed when he was called to go out to a place which he was to receive as an inheritance; and he went out, not knowing where he was to go (Heb. 11:8).

*Both* children and adults have responsibilities and are accountable before God to respond accordingly. Children are told to obey. That is their responsibility—to obey their parents *in the Lord,* for this is right. The Bible does not say that parents will always be right or for children to obey *only* when parents are right. Parents (and teachers) are fallible creatures, they will make mistakes, but they are still to be obeyed. They are to be obeyed, not because they are necessarily right, but as an expression of obedience and love to God.

A question which naturally follows is: Does one blindly obey all commands of those placed in authority? After all, six million Jews died during World War II because of such an assumption. The answer is *no.* One is to obey the commands that are not in conflict with God's directives and norms for conduct. Acts 5:29 states: "But Peter and the apostles answered, 'We must obey God rather than men.' "[2]

Commands that are in conflict with the directives found in Scripture are to be *dis*obeyed (Ex. 1:17; Dan. 3:18). But, as the apostles demonstrated many times, one must also be willing to submit to the consequences of such an act of noncompliance (Acts 5:40-42). One remains under authority. But teachers and parents also have responsibilities in these matters. They are to treat their children in a respectful manner which does not tend to cause resentment of adults and their use of authority. Colossians 3:21 states: "Fathers, do not provoke your children lest they become discouraged." When Christian adults begin reflecting their own subjective desires for their children rather than reflecting the desires and directives outlined in Scripture, children will often react. Youthful styles and customs can be more in conflict with the teachers' or parents' views of good and bad than with norms stated in Scripture. When adults do not understand the nature of children in general and the unique characteristics and needs of their particular children, anger and resentment are fostered. Often adults should do more observing and listening. They should also try to accept their children as unique, separate beings who have freedom to choose and who are being nurtured toward responsible decision-making. The responses based on choice are not to be of the stimulus-response variety, but are to be voluntary and personal. God desires a unique, creative, heartfelt response. Christian adults should ask and accept the same of their children.

Adults placed in authority should expect children to obey them, but they should not expect children to always agree with them. Children should be allowed freedom of expression, the right to disagree, if this can be done in a serious and respectful manner. Teens often seek to question ideas not out of rebellion, but as a means to develop their own views on an issue. But a line must be clearly drawn between questioning ideas and questioning the authority of the person

---

2. The word *obey* here translates the Greek verb *peitharcheō*. That it means the same as *hypakouō* is evident from its use in Titus 3:1.

with the ideas. Respect is a two-way street, and teachers should allow children and young people to exercise their freedom to the extent that they can responsibly handle it. Although pure democracy is not a biblical concept, in reality, the life within the classroom should be more democratic than autocratic. This is the logical conclusion if one reads the explicit statements in Scripture about authority and obedience, but also reads the implicit statements in Scripture about the nature of man and his relationships. In summary, authority is an issue which must be understood and accepted before correction can effectively take place. Authority comes from God and must be exercised in an authoritatively responsible manner. Authority involves having dominion and providing service. The welfare of the person under authority is always of prime importance. There are several reasons for authority. Within these reasons, the issues of freedom and obedience must be dealt with responsibly by both adults and children.

## Chastening

### A. Correction Rather Than Punishment

Chastening, the second part of biblical nurture or discipline, means "correcting" or "redirecting." The emphasis is on future actions, not on past misdeeds. One does not ignore past misdeeds, because they certainly have a bearing on how to promote future actions, but the goal is to produce acceptable and appropriate conduct in the future. That is a difficult concept for many to accept, because most people have been reared in a climate where retribution, punishment for past deeds, was the norm when misbehavior occurred. But Scripture is quite plain that *chastening differs from punishment.*

Chastening has already been defined as a corrective measure which redirects a person along the pathway on which he should be traveling. It is reformative and has personal growth as a goal. Chastening is a means of maturing a person. It is done in love and focuses on the future. Punishment, on the other hand, is a penalty inflicted upon an offender as retribution or payment for misdeeds. It focuses on the past and reflects anger, being an end in itself rather than a means to an end. Penology (which means punishment) has to do with retribution. Hell is punitive and not reformative.

Scripture explains the differences between chastening and punishment:

## 1. Chastening

Blessed is the man whom thou dost chasten, O LORD, and whom thou dost teach out of thy law (Ps. 94:12).

I have heard Ephraim bemoaning, "Thou hast chastened me, and I was chastened, like an untrained calf; bring me back that I may be restored, for thou art the LORD my God. For after I had turned away I repented; and after I was instructed, I smote upon my thigh; I was ashamed, and I was confounded because I bore the disgrace of my youth" (Jer. 31:18, 19).

But when we are judged by the Lord, we are chastened so that we may not be condemned along with the world" (I Cor. 11:32).[3]

## 2. Punishment

Behold, the day of the LORD comes, cruel, with wrath and fierce anger, to make the earth a desolation and to destroy its sinners from it. For the stars of the heavens and their constellations will not give their light; the sun will be dark at its rising and the moon will not shed its light. I will punish the world for its evil, and the wicked for their iniquity; I will put an end to the pride of the arrogant, and lay low the haughtiness of the ruthless (Isa. 13:9-11).

. . . when the Lord Jesus is revealed from heaven with his mighty angels in flaming fire, inflicting vengeance upon those who do not know God and upon those who do not obey the gospel of our Lord Jesus. They shall suffer the punishment of eternal destruction and exclusion from the presence of the Lord and from the glory of his might (II Thess. 1:7-9).[4]

Scripture is quite plain in distinguishing between chastening and punishment. The characteristics of each as carried out by teachers can be described in the following manner.

---

3. See also Revelation 3:19.
4. Also see Matthew 25:46; II Peter 2:9; Jude 6, 7.

|  | *Chastening* | *Punishment* |
|---|---|---|
| *Purpose:* | Redirects toward acceptable and appropriate conduct. A means to an end. | Inflicts a penalty for an offense. An end in itself. |
| *Focus:* | On future, acceptable conduct. | On past, unacceptable conduct. Also on the child's person. |
| *Attitude:* | Reflects love and concern on the part of the teacher. | Reflects hostility, frustration, and possible sadism. |
| *Resulting Emotion in the Child:* | Security. | Fear, guilt, resentment, possible rejection. |

Chastening is *reformative;* punishment is *retributive.* The life and death of Jesus Christ were intended to satisfy divine justice on two counts. Not only did Jesus fulfil God's demand for perfect obedience, but through his death he also paid the penalty for man's failure to render that obedience. When one acknowledges Christ as his Savior, he is no longer liable to punishment. This is reserved for those who do not accept Christ's payment for sin. Scripture bears this out:

> But he was wounded for our transgressions, he was bruised for our iniquities; upon him was the chastisement that made us whole, and with his stripes we are healed (Isa. 53:5).

> But God shows his love for us in that while we were yet sinners Christ died for us. Since, therefore, we are now justified by his blood, much more shall we be saved by him from the wrath of God (Rom. 5:8, 9).

Since God does not inflict avenging punishment upon his children, Scripture seems to indicate that adults should not punish theirs. Punishment, as righteous vengeance, is to be within the jurisdiction of a holy and omniscient God.

> Vengeance is mine, and recompense, for the time when their foot shall slip; for the day of their calamity is at hand, and their doom comes swiftly. For the LORD will vindicate his people and have compassion on his servants, when he sees that their power is gone, and there is none remaining, bond or free (Deut. 32: 35, 36).

> Beloved, never avenge yourselves, but leave it to the wrath of

God; for it is written, "Vengeance is mine, I will repay." And again, "The Lord will judge his people" (Rom. 12:19).[5]

Scripture quite explicitly points out that human beings are prohibited from exacting vengeance, i.e., judgmental punishment, precisely because only God can perfectly judge right and wrong. God alone can judge and exact vengeance; man can only love and chasten (see Rom. 12:9-21).

God does not motivate his children by fear of punishment. In fact, God first removes the threat of punishment; then he asks for the grateful response of obedience. This is the whole point of justification by grace.

> There is therefore now no condemnation for those who are in Christ Jesus. For the gifts and the call of God are irrevocable. . . . I appeal to you therefore, brethren, by the mercies of God, to present your bodies as a living sacrifice, holy and acceptable to God, which is your spiritual worship (Rom. 8:1; 11:29; 12:1).

> There is no fear in love, but perfect love casts out fear. For fear has to do with punishment, and he who fears is not perfected in love (I John 4:18).

Teachers who use punitive control techniques often defend their position by saying that it may not agree with educational or psychological theory, but it certainly works! There are several problems with this line of thinking. First, Christian teachers are to look first of all to Scripture for direction on relationships and nurture. Secondly, doing something simply because it works is pure pragmatism. The Bible instructs man to do what is right. Thirdly, punishment does not teach correct conduct. And, fourthly, fear can motivate one to great activity, but this outward conformity is biblically unacceptable. Love based on inward commitment will produce actions that are acceptable to God.

In summary, the Bible directs adults to correct their children in love, to guide them in the direction which is acceptable to God. The Bible also directs that vengeance or punishment be left to God.

---

5. Also see Hebrews 10:30.

BIBLICAL CHASTENING: "CORRECTIVE" DISCIPLINE     107

## B. Behavior Problems as Opportunities

Christian teachers should not be overly dismayed or discouraged over the presence of problems within the school. The distinctiveness found within the Christian school is not the absence of problems (although, hopefully, through godly instruction, many can be avoided), but in the manner in which they are resolved. *All* schools have problems. Satan takes no holidays and sin is no respecter of persons or places. In fact, as the Book of Job points out, God *allows* Satan to tempt and to try God's people.

Behavior problems can be opportunities for meaningful learning to take place. The manner in which a teacher deals with a problem can contribute much to the nurturing process. Children quickly see how "deep" the personal convictions of the teacher really are. Hypocrisy shows up very nicely under pressure. A Christian adult who can apply biblical principles in a practical manner when the "chips are down" will be sharing a very precious gift with his children. Problems, then, in this sense, should be welcomed (Rom. 5:3-4; II Cor. 12:9, 10; James 1:2, 3).

In the Bible trials are considered to be of value precisely because they can strengthen one's trust in God; they can lead to true spiritual growth. For the Christian teacher, irresponsible conduct by children can be a marvelous opportunity for such spiritual growth, both for him and the children involved.

Conflict within the school, openly acknowledged and dealt with, can be far healthier for children than most adults think. In such situations, children have an opportunity to experience conflict, learn how to cope with it biblically, and, thus, become better prepared to resolve conflicts in a Christ-like manner in later life.

Adults who base their lifestyle on biblical norms are provided a unique opportunity when a child misbehaves. Christian teachers are to respond in a manner which is *abnormal* to that found within secular society. God's ways to solve problems and to heal relationships differ from man's ways. Scripture provides examples of this concept in practice:

> You have heard it said, "You shall love your neighbor and hate your enemy." But I say to you love your enemies and pray for

those who persecute you, so that you may be the sons of your Father who is in heaven; for he makes his sun to rise on the evil and on the good, and sends rain on the just and on the unjust. For if you love those who love you, what reward have you? Do not even the tax collectors do the same? And if you salute only your brethren, what more are you doing than others? Do not even the Gentiles do the same (Matt. 5:43-47)?

Bless those who persecute you; bless and do not curse them. . . . No, "if your enemy is hungry, feed him; if he is thirsty, give him drink; for by so doing you will heap burning coals of fire upon his head." Do not be overcome by evil, but overcome evil with good (Rom. 12:14, 20, 21).

The biblical approach to resolving conflicts and problems should be so radically different and attractive that the children cannot help but recognize the distinctiveness of the Christian life in practice. Teachers are told in Scripture to love the student who is most unlovable. To react with hostility or unkindness is to negate the results of whatever verbal nurturing has taken place.

*     *     *     *     *

The act of chastening cannot be formulated into a blueprint or prescriptive recipe that can neatly fit every situation. Each adult, each child, and each situation is so complex and contains so many variables that no one problem is quite the same as the next. For this reason no attempt is made here to provide extremely well-defined solutions to particular problems. Instead, general principles are offered with the hope that one or a combination of several can be applied to various types of problems. God does not desire to have others solve our problems for us. We are to seek assistance and insight, but biblical principles are to be personally applied to the unique situations that each person faces each day.

The next section of this chapter is divided into three parts. First, general principles are provided for a context within which all corrective procedures should fall. Secondly, suggestions are offered on how to deal with the low-keyed, everyday type of problems, those which need no well-planned, long-range strategy. Finally, suggestions are offered on how to deal with the more serious types of problems, those that are constantly repeating themselves.

## C. Context for Corrective Procedures

All corrective procedures must take place within the framework of firmness and kindness. Corrective measures that are firm demonstrate respect for oneself and for the responsibilities of one placed in authority. Measures that are kind demonstrate respect for others and signify a recognition of the function and nature of children as image-bearers. Within this framework of firmness and kindness are found three principles which should be followed for effective chastening. They are consistency, clarity, and fairness.

First, one must be consistent. He must say what he means and mean what he says. One must not correct according to personal mood, but by prearranged guidelines. An act of disobedience is wrong at any time, no matter what the mood of the adult. God has given man guidelines by which to live. Whenever these guidelines are ignored, consequences occur—consistently. Consistency means dealing with small infractions. This will often deter larger problems. Consistency also means that teachers are to follow up on their requests or commands. Adults often become sidetracked and fail to determine whether or not children have complied with a request or order. Children usually respond in direct proportion to the consistency of the adult.

A second principle is that of clarity. The expectations or rules must be clear from the very beginning. Children cannot be held accountable for that which they have not been told or have not understood. When irresponsible behavior is exhibited, the child should be informed quite precisely of the nature of the problem. It is possible that he either was not aware of his behavior or did not consider it to be unacceptable by the teacher. Children often view things in a manner which is different from that of adults. When an adult explains his reason for concern, a child is provided an opportunity for the additional insight necessary both for learning and for the actions based on that learning. Clarity, then, is an important prerequisite to self-discipline.

The third principle is that of fairness. The corrective measures must fit both the nature and the seriousness of the misdeed. The correction should provide the insight and the assistance necessary for the child to find redirection. It should, then, possess a logical relationship to the irresponsible behavior that took place and to its responsible counterpart. Also, correction should not be of greater severity than the misdeed warrants, since that could produce a feeling of unfairness which might tend to expand the problem. Both the seriousness of the misconduct and the attitude behind the act, as best as can be determined, should have a bearing on the corrective measures taken. The corrective measures must also fit the person. Some children need a greater amount of corrective influence or a more distinctive form than others. Corrective measures that do not reflect the uniqueness of the individual often will be ineffective. On the other hand, personalized discipline can be a vehicle for communicating love and concern, and for developing effective redirection.

A teacher ought also to be aware of something called the "ripple effect." This often occurs within a classroom immediately after correction has taken place. The effects spread out like concentric wavelets of influence from the child who was corrected to those classmates who were witnesses to the episode. This can have a positive, exemplary effect; but the ripple effect can also have negative results. The use of highly emotional threats by a teacher usually causes children to lower their estimation of his helpfulness, likeability, and fairness. It tends to produce a great deal of distracting behavior and will probably impair the total learning experience. Attempting to see oneself through the eyes of a child, and recognizing ahead of time the effect of one's actions on children, can be helpful to the teacher in the correcting process.

Finally, when inappropriate behavior occurs within a classroom, a teacher ought to consider a few things before reacting. Obviously, for the more experienced teacher, this type of consideration usually happens instinctively and within a split second.

1. He should determine whether or not the incident is worth reacting to. Is it an annoyance only to the teacher? Is it hindering the progress toward meeting the educational goals?

2. He should not lose his entire class or lesson for one person. If at all possible, the problem should be resolved without "missing

a beat" in the lesson. Put the immediate "fire" out so that the class can continue functioning. Follow up, if necessary, should be dealt with at a more appropriate time.

3. Quiet, firm, decisive action is always more effective than threats.
4. He should remain cool and objective. The handling of a problem must not be viewed as a personal vendetta but as a natural or logical action. It should be as non-threatening as possible.
5. If the situation calls for humor or laughter with the children, he should try it.

### D. Corrective Procedures for Minor Incidents

1. First, nonverbal signs can be given. They may be used individually or combined.
   a. Look at the person until he stops his inappropriate behavior.
   b. Use fingers for direction. Examples are:
      — a finger placed on the lips means "be quiet."
      — a finger pointed toward the student's book means "start reading."
   c. Use silence. If the teacher is reading or speaking to the class, he can stop until the person or persons who are talking or not paying attention become conscious of their behavior.
   d. Use bodily position by moving closer to the student creating the problem. A non-threatening touch or tap on a younger student's shoulder can be effective.
2. Secondly, if additional measures are needed, verbal messages can be sent.
   a. Simply call the student's name and then use a non-verbal cue for direction.
   b. Call the person by name, explain what he is doing that is inappropriate, and give direction on what he *should* be doing. (Some would omit the third part of this message out of respect for the student in the belief that the student should be allowed the opportunity to choose appropriate behavior without being told.) Often a teacher's voice will naturally rise and his speech will become more rapid when a problem is being dealt with. The opposite has a more calming effect. If any-

thing, a teacher's voice should lower and the rate of speech should become more deliberate.

c. Conflicts and confrontations can often be temporarily defused by sending a student the message that one "hears what he is saying" and "knows how he feels." This type of empathetic listening must be followed up in a more complete way at a later, more appropriate time.

3. Finally, action can be taken.

a. Move the student to a part of the room in which reinforcement of the inappropriate behavior is not present. This could be a prearranged location of which the students are aware. A student could be assigned there until the lesson ends, until the teacher has had an opportunity to speak with him, or until the student believes that he can handle himself in a more responsible manner.

b. Ask the student to wait outside the room until the teacher has an opportunity to speak with him. Moving the student to the hall for a brief conference keeps the matter private, contained, and non-humiliating—all characteristics which tend to foster cooperation rather than hostility and rebellion. It is also respectful and biblical. Matthew 18:15 says: "If your brother sins against you, go and tell him his fault between you and him alone. If he listens to you, you have gained your brother." When the teacher *does* take time to speak with him, a question such as, "Why do you think I sent you out?" can establish a non-threatening rapport. It allows the child to explain his actions from his perspective and also allows him the opportunity to evaluate his own actions. The teacher can, in addition, gain insight into the perceptions and attitude of the student so that corrective measures can be appropriately selected.

c. If a student cannot control himself, he should be asked, or allowed of his own volition, to go to an assigned area to cool off. He could return either under his own volition or at a time determined by the teacher. An important point must be made here. In many schools students are sent to the principal or to the guidance counselor, who is supposed to resolve these teacher-student conflicts, even though one member of the conflict, namely, the teacher, is not present. Often the principal or counselor assumes the child is at fault. This is grossly unfair and unbiblical. The two parties of a conflict are to attempt to resolve their differences between the two of them. If this seems impossible, they must follow the injunction of Matthew 18:16: "But if he does not listen, take one or two others along with you, that every word may be confirmed by the evidence of two or three witnesses." The principal and/or guidance counselor can be called in as advisors, arbitrators, or witnesses only after the teacher and student have first attempted to resolve their problem and have failed. There are practical reasons for this approach as well. If a teacher and a student are to function effectively together within a classroom, genuine healing must have taken place. Also, it is possible that the teacher may have been the party in the wrong. Assuming the student is always guilty is both disrespectful and unrealistic. Healing and cooperation cannot take place within an atmosphere that lacks a sense of justice.

Before moving on to suggestions for correcting the more serious behavior problems, one other dimension of chastening should be discussed. Care must be taken to focus on solutions to problems rather than to debate the issue of who was to blame for the problem. The question to be asked is: "What can be done to redirect this student so that he can begin acting responsibly of his own volition?" Emphasis is to be placed more on future actions than on past misconduct. Teachers and students can easily become so bogged down with attempts to determine blame for misdeeds that they lose sight of how to promote more responsible behavior in the future. This should not be surprising, since the second recorded sin of mankind was that of Adam blaming Eve for his misconduct. Man has been seeking deterministic and causistic answers for his behavior ever since. It frees him of personal responsibility and, thus, of accountability. But that does not reflect the nature of man, for he is responsible, has freedom to choose, and he is accountable. A person's actions are a direct result of his will, and, thus, he is personally accountable. Personal blame must be accepted for one's irresponsible conduct. Plans can then be made for acting in a more responsible manner in the future.

## E. Corrective Solutions for Major Problems

Problems that repeat themselves frequently can be considered to be major. They are not incidental or unplanned. Major problems are of the habitual or long-term variety. In daily practice, however, these problems and suggested solutions cannot be divided so neatly. Many happen simultaneously and, perhaps, with the same child. Hopefully, teachers can use the information provided here to devise their own plan of action for their own particular situations.

Continuing with the goal of correction or redirection, the suggestions that follow may be placed within three categories: first, taking no action; second, taking "positive" action; thirdly, taking "negative" action.

## 1. Taking No Action

It is evident in Scripture that God often *allows* people to learn that all choices bear consequences:

> Behold, the wicked man conceives evil, and is pregnant with mischief, and brings forth lies. He makes a pit, digging it out, and falls into the hole which he has made. His mischief returns upon his own head, and on his own pate his violence descends (Ps. 7:14-16).

> Therefore God gave them up in the lusts of their hearts to impurity, to the dishonoring of their bodies among themselves, because they exchanged the truth about God for a lie and worshipped and served the creature rather than the creator . . . (Rom. 1:24-25).

> Do not be deceived; God is not mocked, for whatever a man sows, that he will also reap. For he who sows to the Spirit will from the Spirit reap eternal life (Gal. 6:7-8).[6]

The parable of the prodigal son in Luke 15:11-24 provides an example of natural consequences for one's actions being used as a

---

6. Also see Proverbs 22:8; Matthew 26:52; II Thessalonians 3:10.

teaching device. Every sin has some harmful effect on one's life. Some results of sin are obvious; others are more subtle. Whatever the case, allowing natural consequences to help redirect behavior has much in its favor, including the fact that it teaches accountability and promotes the development of self-discipline.

Sometimes it is best to allow "nature to take its course" and to allow a child to suffer the natural consequences of his actions. Natural consequences are based on the natural flow of events and are those which take place without adult interference. One could ask himself, "What would happen if I didn't interfere?" Obviously, there are some circumstances in which the child's safety would be endangered and natural consequences would have to be curtailed.

The behavioristic principle of *satiation* is similar in some ways to natural consequences. The satiation principle states that to stop a child from acting in a particular way, one may allow him to continue performing the undesired act until he tires of it. The hope is that a child will become satiated with the consequences of his behavior because of boredom or fatigue. This view of natural consequences seems to depart a bit from the biblical model which seeks to have the individual gain insight into his misconduct as evaluated against biblical norms. Satiation carries with it implications of stimulus-response, which does not necessarily include insight.

One other behavioristic approach which calls for no action is *extinction*. It states that to stop a child from acting in a particular way, one arranges conditions so that he receives no rewards or reinforcement following an undesirable act. This, too, can be dealt with on a purely stimulus-response level which does not do justice to a biblical view of man. But extinction has certain applications which appear to be biblically acceptable. It might be appropriate for the teacher to ignore certain behaviors which are meant to "bait" him (such as foot tapping) and to deal with the attitudes demonstrated at a later time. Perhaps certain obnoxious behavior can rightly be ignored by parents, teachers, and students with the hope that it will extinguish itself through lack of reinforcement, but Christians must not ignore another person who is by his actions saying, "I need attention; I need someone to care about me."

## 2. Taking "Positive" Action

If a child fails to learn from his mistakes and thus fails to redirect his own behavior, the teacher must take steps to assist the child in this process. One of these is the application of logical consequences for his actions. Logical consequences, reflecting biblical and societal norms, are a means of teaching a child that there are certain rules in life that people live by. They should be logical, in other words, fit the misbehavior. Logical consequences are usually planned by the teacher, but there can be participation by the child. They are often arranged ahead of time, so that children are well aware of the consequences of their actions. Although it is the teacher who is responsible for what takes place, he acts not as a powerful authority but as a representative of an order which affects all in a similar manner. This adds a dimension of objectivity to a situation which might easily bog down in personalities and emotions rather than issues.

The use of logical consequences seems to be in harmony with general principles in Scripture. The fact that consequences for behavior are structured in advance reflects both harmony with the biblical view of authority and with the biblical view of man as one who is responsible and must bear the consequences of his actions. Logical consequences that are related to the deed also tend to emphasize behavior change rather than question the worth and dignity of the individual.

One form of logical consequences is restitution. Restitution was a vital part of Jewish law and tradition. Exodus 22:1 states that "if a man steals an ox or a sheep and kills it or sells it, he shall pay five oxen for an ox, and four sheep for a sheep. He shall make restitution." That law was obeyed by Zacchaeus after he came to know Christ: "Behold, Lord, the half of my goods I give to the poor; and if I have defrauded anyone of anything, I restore it fourfold" (Luke 19:8). Restitution continues to be a valid part of biblical correction. It should take place when a misdeed involves another person and his property. If one steals or damages another's property, he should return or restore it. If one does an unacceptable job on a task, he should do it over again in an acceptable manner. If time is misused, it should be used properly at some other time in a make-up session. An act of disobedience must be corrected by obeying the request that was made. If a child speaks to an adult (or to another child) in a manner that is unacceptable, he should repeat himself in a more acceptable way. An act of disrespect can be corrected by means of an apology or by repeating the act in a courteous manner. Hurting another person calls for at least an apology. Restitution of this type requires a person to undo what he has done as part of the redirective or corrective process.

Another form of logical consequences is withdrawal or isolation. When the people of Israel did not honor their covenantal relationship, God would withdraw his blessing from them until such a time as they would repent. Deuteronomy 31:16-17 records:

> . . . This people will rise and play the harlot after the strange gods of the land, where they go to be among them, and they will forsake me and break my covenant which I have made with them. Then my anger will be kindled against them in that day, and I will forsake them and hide my face from them, and they will be devoured; and many evils and troubles will come upon them, so that they will say in that day, "Have not these evils come upon us because our God is not among us?"

Following the same concept of separation but within a different context, the teacher should isolate any individuals who cannot function in a socially acceptable manner within the group. If one cannot keep his part of the social contract that places man in interrelation and interdependence with other men, he should be isolated until he is willing to change his actions. Sin and open rebellion in Scripture ultimately resulted in excommunication from the body after the proper confrontations took place and repentance was not evident.

> I appeal to you, brethren, to take note of those who create dissensions and difficulties, in opposition to the doctrine which you have been taught; avoid them (Rom. 16:17).

> Now we command you, brethren, in the name of our Lord Jesus Christ, that you keep away from any brother who is living in idleness and not in accord with the tradition that you received from us. . . . If any one refuses to obey what we say in this letter, note that man, and have nothing to do with him, that he may be

ashamed. Do not look on him as an enemy, but warn him as a brother (II Thess. 3:6, 14, 15).

This separation or isolation can be taken in progressive steps (Matt. 18:15-17). There may be a special place within the classroom away from the other students that would take care of most of the problems. The school might also designate a special room for persons who cannot control themselves within the classroom. The next step would be to send the child home.

Restoration to the group and growth in self-discipline, however, must always be the goals. This is evident in the advice Paul gave to the Corinthian church:

> Let him who has done this be removed from among you . . . you are to deliver this man to Satan for the destruction of the flesh, that his spirit may be saved in the day of the Lord Jesus Christ (I Cor. 5:2, 5).

The person must always be given the opportunity to try to function with the others. The teacher would have to be the judge of whether or not the student had a change of heart and was truly committed to his new choice of behavior.

A third form of logical consequences is the withdrawal of certain privileges if the child cannot properly handle them.

God denied Adam and Eve access to the garden of Eden after they were irresponsible with their freedom (Gen. 2:23-24). He refused to allow Eli's sons to become priests when they misused the trust placed in them (I Sam. 2:31-36). King David was denied the privilege of keeping the son born to Bathsheba and him because of their sin (II Sam. 12:15-23).

The withdrawal of privileges could be applied after the irresponsible use of physical education or art equipment.[7] If a child is not responsible on safety patrol, the privilege can be withdrawn until such a time as he and the teacher both believe that he would be responsible.

---

7. This choice of examples is not to indicate that physical education and art are "fun" activities and less important than other subjects. It is just that whatever is withdrawn should have been viewed as a privilege *by the student*, and these two subjects often are.

Logical consequences are effective *only* if they are applied consistently. They can be used effectively only when a good relationship exists between the teacher and the child. In a power conflict they are viewed as punishment.

Logical consequences for one's actions can help to avoid power struggles; they can teach personal responsibility; they can help to eliminate unnecessary warning, nagging, and correction. But they also have their limitations. Unless the child can gain insight into his actions and have a heartfelt commitment toward redirection, logical consequences are nothing more than external devices for changing one's behavior.

\* \* \* \* \*

A behavioristic principle which falls under the category of "positive" action is that of *incompatible alternatives*. This states that to stop a child from acting in a particular way, one may reward or reinforce an alternative action that is inconsistent with or cannot be performed at the same time as the undesired act. Examples of this principle in action are the appointment of a litterbug as the leader of an anti-litter committee or the appointment of a playground bully as a member of the playground safety patrol. Once again, if insight and commitment to change are absent, the change in behavior is strictly superficial. However, this technique could be used with the foreknowledge of the individual who has the problem. A child who has difficulty listening to others during committee meetings might be appointed chairman with the responsibility to see to it that all opinions are heard on an issue. A disruptive child might be invited to teach a lesson to experience the difficulty of teaching while children are misbehaving. And, to counter the adage that "idle hands are the devil's playthings," one could make certain that those idle hands have plenty of worthwhile things to do.

### 3. Taking "Negative" Action

Quotation marks are placed around the words "positive" and "negative" solely because of the difference in the way they are likely to be perceived by the children to whom they are to be applied. *The goal remains positive, to redirect the child in the way he should be going.*

Hopefully, the child receives this message and feels loved in the process. That is, at times, a difficult message for the teacher to convey, especially as more drastic corrective actions are considered. There are two approaches which fall under this category—the behavioristic technique of *negative reinforcement,* and the use of corporal punishment.

The principle of negative reinforcement states that to stop a child from acting a particular way, one may arrange for him to terminate a mildly unpleasant situation by improving his behavior. The unpleasant situation should fit the behavior to be changed. Justice and logic would seem to dictate that there should be a relationship between the two. The imposition of "negative" activities on a child while granting the option to "escape" from those negative activities through improved behavior is essentially what negative reinforcement is all about. It differs from punishment, which would be the imposition of a penalty to be inflicted and terminated without regard to future changes in behavior. Punishment is retribution for past misdeeds. An example of negative reinforcement is the use of the "time out room." This is an area to which a child can go voluntarily when he realizes, first, that his behavior is becoming undesirable and, secondly, that he needs a place to settle down and prepare for re-entry into the group situation. The teacher can also send a child to such a location when his behavior becomes socially unacceptable. The child is allowed to rejoin the group when he decides that he is willing to control himself in a socially responsible manner.

Negative reinforcement seems to be usable for the Christian, but, once again, there are precautions which should be noted. A change in behavior without a corresponding change in attitude is not an acceptable goal. If the only reason a child improves his conduct is to avoid an uncomfortable situation, then his motivation is biblically unacceptable.

The other "negative" action which a teacher can take following misconduct by a child has traditionally been called *corporal punishment,* meaning paddling, whipping, or spanking. Assuming that the spanking of a child as a form of punishment is wrong, based on previously stated arguments (see pp. 103-106), what about using spanking as a part of the *chastening* or *correcting* process? A study of the Bible reveals that there may be a place for spanking. Practically all references to the use of the rod to correct a child occur in Proverbs:

> He who spares the rod hates his son, but he who loves him is diligent to discipline him (Prov. 13:24).

> Folly is bound up in the heart of a child, but the rod of discipline drives it far from him (Prov. 22:15).

> Do not withhold discipline from a child; if you beat him with a rod, he will not die. If you beat him with the rod you will save his life from Sheol (Prov. 23:13, 14).

> The rod and reproof give wisdom, but a child left to himself brings shame to his mother (Prov. 29:15).

There is no doubt that these references support the directive stated many times in Scripture that parents are to correct their children from wrongdoing. The use of the word *rod* certainly indicates that nurture and discipline are to take place. But whether the use of the word rod also indicates that the form of correction is to be a spanking is less certain. There are a few cautionary notes that one should make before establishing that as a rigid conclusion.

First, the Book of Proverbs is written in the form of Hebrew poetry, a form that often uses vivid imagery. In other Old Testament books there are uses of *shebet,* the Hebrew word for "rod," which obviously call for a symbolic interpretation of rod:

> Oh, Assyria, the rod of my anger, the staff of my fury (Isa. 10:5)!

> . . . and he shall smite the earth with the rod of his mouth . . . (Isa. 11:4).

> I am the man who has seen affliction under the rod of his wrath (Lam. 3:1).

Usually one would look to the context for a clearer understanding of a word, but the Book of Proverbs provides no such context for the use of the word *rod*. For the most part, the individual proverbs stand alone, unrelated to those which precede and follow. One must be cautious, then, about translating these references to the word *rod* as commands to physically correct a child. They are, indeed, commands to chasten or redirect him, but to be more specific than that is to read into the texts that which is not necessarily there.

Secondly, all references to using the rod on children are found in the Old Testament. The Greek word for rod, *rhabdos,* is used eleven times in the New Testament and never to command the physical correction or the spanking of children. Indeed, *rhabdos* is used very meaningfully in I Corinthians 4:21, where it obviously symbolizes chastening as a general directive to follow rather than as a specific endorsement of spanking.

While Proverbs does instruct, then, *that* correction must be exercised, it gives no clear command as to *how* it should be done. On the whole, the Bible teaches that genuine chastening or correction is that which attempts to return the person to the proper way of life. That is what teachers have the responsibility to do, and, with the guidance of the Holy Spirit, they can use whatever means will effectively and lovingly accomplish that end.

Scripture often encourages actions of moderation. The moderate and wise use of spanking is certainly within biblical freedom. It is the misuse of physical correction that is biblically unacceptable. Child beating is on the increase across North America, within both secular and Christian situations. The tensions of life are being felt more and more, and, consequently, misuse of spanking is becoming an area for increased concern. Some adults, quite frankly, are emotionally unable to administer physical correction in a moderate and wise manner. It would be best for them to ban it totally from their options.

For those adults who believe that moderate and wise use of spanking is acceptable and can be handled by them, the following suggestions are meant to be helpful:

a. Be certain that spanking is the most appropriate means of correction available. In most circumstances it should be near the bottom of the list of options—"when all else fails!"

b. Be certain that the spanking is being used as a means to "redirect the child in the way he should go" and not as a punishment for past misdeeds.

c. Be sensitive to the effects of a spanking on particular children. For some children a spanking tends to instill an unhealthy fear of the person administering the spanking.

    d.  Don't spank when you are out of control.  If a spanking in your judgment is warranted, it will be just as warranted when you calm down.  There will be less chance of a severe beating taking place; there will be more likelihood that loving correction will be the result.

    e.  Physical correction is better "understood" by younger children than is reasoning; thus, spanking has more validity and effect with younger children than with older children.

    f.  Use your hand rather than an instrument, so that you, too, can can feel the power of your strength.

    g.  Strike only the child's bottom.  Striking a child elsewhere can easily cause bodily harm.  Striking a child across the face can cause psychological damage.

    h.  Be certain that both you and your child feel the love which must be present within biblical discipline.

### Summary and Conclusions

Biblical nurture or discipline begins with instruction, but it also includes correction.  Before such correction takes place, however, it is best to have a clear picture of the scriptural view of authority.  Authority comes from God and must be carried out by man in an authoritative manner.  Authority is practiced by having dominion and by being of service.  For authority to function properly, the concepts of freedom, honor, and obedience must be understood.

Correction differs from punishment.  Correction looks forward to a change in behavior.  It is reformative.  Punishment is retributive.  It serves as a penalty for a past deed.  Christ has borne the punishment for his children.  Punishment can be rightly administered only by God.

There are many different ways to correct, some very simple, others that are of greater magnitude.  Self-correction is the ideal, and allowing natural consequences to redirect behavior should be considered.  External application of logical consequences seems to be the other most acceptable form of redirection usable by the Christian teacher.  Physical correction has a legitimate but limited place.

All correcting must be conducted within the framework of kindness.  It must be consistent, clear, and fair.  It must be done in love.

## Chapter 5

# Biblical Counseling: The Act of Healing

## Introduction

". . . fathers, . . . bring up [your children] in the nurture and admonition of the Lord" (Eph. 6:4).

The responsibility of teachers and parents for the attitudes and conduct of their children is threefold. The word *nurture* (discipline) in Ephesians 6:4 carries with it two connotations—instruction and correction, directives which were dealt with in the preceding two chapters. The third directive is found in the word *admonition* (KJV) or *instruction* (RSV). Actually, the paraphrase found in the Living Bible more nearly explains the meaning of this word: ". . . bring them up with the loving discipline the Lord himself approves, with suggestions and godly advice."

The word *admonition* used in Ephesians 6:4 is the Greek word *noutheteō/nouthesia*. This is a word used for counseling and implies that scriptural direction is being given. Admonition includes counsel, warning, and gentle or friendly reproof.[1] Several other Scripture passages which use the word *noutheteō/nouthesia* can shed further light on its meaning:

> I myself am satisfied about you, my brethren, that you yourselves are full of goodness, filled with all knowledge, and able to instruct one another (Rom. 15:14).

Now these things happened to them as a warning, but they were

---

1. A counsellor is more than an advice giver, however. He is one who attempts to help people to help themselves. As has been stated over and over in the previous chapters, adults must first communicate love and respect, which serves as a proper context or setting for openness in relationships and for a change in attitudes and conduct. Unless children and young people can feel a genuine concern on the part of the helping adult, no trust will be given and no real progress will be made.

written down for our instruction, upon whom the end of the ages has come (I Cor. 10:11).

Let the word of Christ dwell in you richly, teach and admonish one another in all wisdom, and sing psalms and hymns and spiritual songs with thankfulness in your hearts to God (Col. 3:16).

But we beseech you, brethren, to respect those who labor among you and are over you in the Lord and admonish you (I Thess. 5:12).

Do not look upon him as an enemy, but warn him as a brother (II Thess. 3:15).

As for a man who is factious, after admonishing him once or twice, have nothing more to do with him (Titus 3:10).

Adults are not to limit their usage to *either* nurture (instruction and correction) *or* admonition (counseling); they are told to *both* nurture *and* admonish their children. And even though instruction, correction, and counseling are logically applied in that order, often the directives are to be carried out simultaneously. The three are a unified, mutually supporting trio. Instruction is a continuous process, with, perhaps, a higher degree of concentration to take place when the children are at a younger age. Correction takes place whenever it is necessary. Some correction will probably be necessary at various times while the counseling process is taking place, especially if the counseling occurs over a long period of time. In other words, instruction, correction, and counseling are a *unity*. They are interrelated and interdependent. They are not meant to be separated in essence or in time.

Admonition differs from nurture, however, in some very important ways. It is to be used in a manner and to a degree which is appropriate to the maturity of the child and to the situation being dealt with. As children grow older and more mature, several changes gradually take place. Young children, up to ages seven and eight, are often unable to have genuine understanding or insight into their own misbehavior. Therefore, reasoning with them often ends in failure. The reason for this is that they are quite stimulus-response or pleasure-pain oriented at that young age. Very young children connect right and wrong with the results of their actions. Right actions are followed by praise or rewards; wrong actions are followed by scolding or pain. Corrective procedures are to be used which keep these facts in mind. As they mature, children grow in personal moral consciousness; they become more personally responsible—able to respond in a thoughtful manner—and, thus, they become more personally accountable for their actions as well. Growth in personal understanding, responsibility, and accountability all increase in direct proportion. Children gradually move to a more responsible level of development and growth, but this next level or period of time in their lives is, in turn, quite legalistic. They understand the difference between right and wrong to a greater degree than they did at a younger age. Children of elementary school age are usually within a stage of development that could be called *moral realism*. Even though the pleasure-pain aspect of motivation remains with them (adults continue to possess this element of motivation as well), children gain a greater degree of understanding into the issue of morality (right or wrong) as they mature. Elementary age youngsters see issues as being right or wrong without much gray, middle area for debate. Children who are at the stage of moral realism tend to apply the letter of the law, a rigid "no exceptions" interpretation to moral and ethical questions. No allowances are made for circumstances.

But children usually begin moving into the stage of *moral relativism* around age twelve, give or take a few years. Rather than concentrating on the *letter* of the law, children and young people in this stage of development or growth seem to focus on the *spirit* of the law. Circumstances are taken into account, and the individual's intent is deemed to be of greater importance than the act and its consequences. A flexible "no rule is sacred" interpretation is often given to issues. Such children have gained the ability to think in an abstract manner in addition to the previously acquired ability to think in a concrete manner. Rather than possessing the ability to mentally cope with only two variables (e.g., right and wrong) at one time, they can now cope with several variables at the same time. Issues become more complex. There are fewer simple solutions to the problems of life.

Moral relativism should not be confused with situation ethics.

Moral relativism can operate within certain norms or absolutes such as "love God." Situation ethics lacks norms and is an existential, man-centered, do-your-own-thing basis for conduct.

Not every young person or adult functions within the stage of moral relativism with any great degree of success. Some remain very legalistic in their outlook most of their lives. Issues are simply black or white, right or wrong. Other people, more hedonistic in outlook, seem to reflect the pleasure-pain stage. But, whatever the case, all adults have the ability to function to some degree within all three stages of moral and ethical development.

To summarize, the point to be made is that children, young people, and adults are unique and are to be treated as such. Personal growth takes place gradually over a period of time. The degree to which one uses instruction, correction, or counseling depends greatly on the maturity of the person being dealt with.

Instruction (what should be) is a continuing process; correction (restorative action) and counseling (restorative communication), however, should take place in various degrees. Both are needed, but depending on the maturity of the child and the particular situation, the degree of usage differs.

*Example One* —Minor offenses or misconduct can be handled primarily through the use of low-key corrective measures. The ratio of correction to counseling might be 90:10.

*Example Two* —Serious offenses by young children can also be handled more through corrective measures than through counseling because of their levels of moral and ethical development. They are quite behavioristic or legalistic in their outlook. Their development in understanding and insight is limited. But children of elementary school age *do* have a degree of understanding, and a corresponding degree of counseling can be quite productive for a behavior change based on heart commitment. The ratio of correction to counseling might be 70:30.

*Example Three* —Serious offenses by older children and by young people can be handled by placing a greater emphasis on counseling than on correction. Since the goal is "redirection of future conduct," severe corrective measures, which may appear as a "power play" to the young person, may be counter productive. The problem must be dealt with immediately so as to defuse the situation, true, but the redirection may have to take the form of admonition more than a severe form of chastening. Admonition should take place at a later time, when rationality can balance emotions, when the place and time are more conducive for a meaningful exchange. The ratio of correction to counseling might be 30:70.

*Example Four* —Long-terms offenses which reflect maladjustment or emotional problems need a degree of corrective action, but the emphasis must be placed on counseling. The ratio of correction to counseling might be 10:90.

Obviously, examples such as these are general and provide only a "feel" for the concept being considered. The examples also presuppose an ideal situation in which a child received a high concentration of instruction at a young age and the corresponding degree of correction. A child must know the truth before he can be expected to act on the truth.

All four examples are working on a continuum, with correction (restorative action) on the one side and with counseling (restorative communication) on the other:

| *Chastening/Correction* | *Admonition/Counseling* |
|---|---|
| 1. Younger children | 1. Young people |
| 2. Age of moral realism | 2. Age of moral relativism |
| 3. Pleasure-pain/legalism | 3. Understanding/reason |
| 4. One-sided correction | 4. Mutual correction |
| 5. Limited personal responsibility | 5. Greater degree of personal responsibility |
| 6. Reliance on adult (external) direction | 6. Reliance on (internal) self-direction |
| 7. Adult sharing accountability for conduct | 7. More personal accountability for conduct |

As the child become older and more accountable for his actions, the emphasis shifts from left to right. The transition will, of course, be a gradual one, occurring at various rates depending upon the persons and circumstances. And at no time does a person work exclusively with one or the other extreme of the continuum. To some degree both correction and counseling are *always* needed. Both misconduct and the correction that follows can strain relationships and alienate people. Correction provided in love does much to heal relationships, but often additional attention must be given by the teacher involved. Young children usually experience less difficulty in "getting back to normal" than do young people. A hug or some other message of love and acceptance is all a young child often needs. The past is quickly forgotten. Adolescents experience more difficulty, however. A simple hug does not necessarily suffice. A more reasoned, understandable follow-up to corrective actions is advisable. The admonition (restorative counseling) that follows chastening (restorative correction) must often take the form of communicating on a person-to-person basis with the dual purposes of reconciliation and restoration. These are, in fact, the goals of biblical admonition, no matter what form it may take.

Paul writes of such reconciliation:

> Let him who has done this be removed from among you . . . that his spirit may be saved in the day of the Lord Jesus (I Cor. 5:2, 5).

> [Correct] opponents with gentleness. God may perhaps grant that they will repent and come to know the truth, and they may escape from the snare of the devil, after having been captured by him to do his will (II Tim. 2:25-26).

Daniel 4:28-37, in turn, provides a biblical model for restoration. Because Nebuchadnezzar was too proud to recognize the sovereignty of God, his Master drove him out from among his fellow men to live like a wild beast. That motivated him to acknowledge God's supreme rule, which allowed for his reconciliation to God. And then, in verse 36, we are told of his resultant restoration.

> At the same time my reason returned to me; and for the glory of my kingdom, my majesty and splendor returned to me. My counselors and my lords sought me, and I was established in my kingdom and still more greatness was added to me.

A person who, through his conduct, is in disharmony or out of relationship with God, himself, or his fellow man must be brought to harmonious and reconciled relationships. Once reconciliation takes place, restoration must be a resultant action. A person whose actions caused separation to take place must be restored to his former position. When a person has wandered from the pathway which God has ordained as being the correct one, he must be returned to the appointed place and headed in the proper direction. Then, often, only time is needed for the fullness of healing to take place.

The dual goals of reconciliation and restoration are reached by way of a three-stage counseling process. First, there must be confrontation; secondly, confession; and thirdly, covenanting.

### Confrontation

The first step in biblical counseling is confrontation. The person whose conduct is either inappropriate or unacceptable must be made aware of this fact. Matthew 5:23-24 tells what a person should do if someone is offended by him:

> So if you are offering your gift at the altar, and there remember that your brother has something against you, leave your gift there before the altar and go; first be reconciled to your brother, and then come and offer your gift.

Matthew 18:15, on the other hand, gives direction on what to do if one is offended by another person:

> If your brother sins against you, go and tell him his fault, between you and him alone.

In both cases, the person under biblical conviction is to go to the other in Christian confrontation so that the problem can be resolved. Were a problem to arise within the classroom, a teacher who operates on biblical norms would go to the student or students involved and attempt to find a solution to the difficulty.

Man was meant to be in balanced and harmonious relationship. When the conduct of another person either weakens or breaks that relationship, effort must be made for reconciliation and restoration. The relationship becomes imbalanced when one party imposes his will upon the relationship without regard for the needs of the other party. The relationship lacks harmony when one party seeks dominion rather than service. Confrontation must take place in most cases before relationships can be strengthened and restored. People must be made aware of their responsibilities toward maintaining these relationships.

Teachers are not to be passive victims of their students' misconduct. They are directed by Scripture to confront their children on such matters. They, the more mature party in the relationship, are placed in a position of responsible guidance and authority. They must honestly attempt to overlook any personal feelings of alienation and hostility and take concrete steps toward reconciliation. The first such step is confrontation. Avoidance of a problem seldom works, since avoidance often serves as an encouragement for further misconduct, which places further strains on the relationships. It is also entirely possible that the offending party is unaware of the negative effect his conduct is having on the relationship.

But, there is confrontation and there is confrontation! Biblical confrontation is done in genuine love! This love must be felt by the giver and the receiver. A loving confrontation includes the wisdom to know what should be said and what should remain unsaid. Including non-essential information can confuse the issue and can, in fact, further weaken relationships. Persons should not have a burden placed on them which they are not equipped to handle. The sharing of information that people are not emotionally prepared to handle does no one any good. As truthful as certain messages are, they may tend to overwhelm or shatter a person, and such sharing or confrontation may have selfish connotations. The person doing the sharing may feel relieved, but the recipient may have unnecessarily been given a problem which hindered the act of healing rather than helped. The sharing of such information must be seeking the goal of establishing or strengthening a relationship, or it should not be shared at all. Truthfulness is essential in a healthy relationship, but love must *always* remain "the greatest" (I Cor. 13:13). Caution must be taken, then, that only the information necessary to resolve the problem be shared.

The teacher who confronts a young person should send certain non-verbal messages along with the verbal ones. The messages are: "I am willing to become involved with you. I want the involvement to be warm, personal, and friendly. But most important, I desire the involvement to be unconditional and long term. By unconditional I mean that no conditions are imposed. You are accepted as you are, even though I cannot accept your behavior. By long term I mean that I plan to stick with you through thick or thin. You will not be abandoned or rejected." Such messages, sent in ways that are as personal as the teacher sending them, are love personified. It is the same message that the redeemed have received from their Redeemer Jesus Christ.

Confrontation for the purpose of helping another person to become aware of his behavior can take place in various ways. If chastening took place, then a follow-up session for additional restoration in the form of counseling is quite natural. In fact, such an appointment should be made when the problem occurs, so that breaks in relationships are promptly and properly dealt with. If no chastening or correction took place, an appointment can still be arranged. Such statements as, "I've got a problem that I'd like to talk over with you," or, "There is something that has been concerning me that I'd like to share with you," can acquaint the student with your desire for such a session. Natural conversation, genuine interest, gentle probing with questions are other acceptable approaches to getting the topic of one's conduct out in the open for objective discussion. Confrontation is not easy. In fact, it is one of the most difficult actions which God requires of people. But it is biblical, and it is necessary if reconciliation and restoration are to take place.

## Confession

Confrontation is to be followed by confession. Scripture emphasizes the necessity for such confession.

> He who conceals his transgressions will not prosper, but he who confesses and forsakes them will obtain mercy (Prov. 28:13).

> Therefore, confess your sins to one another, and pray for one another, that you may be healed (James 5:16).

> If we say we have no sin, we deceive ourselves, and the truth is

not in us. If we confess our sins, he is faithful and just, and will forgive our sins and cleanse us from all unrighteousness (I John 1:8-9).

It is clear that when one wrongs another, he not only sins against that individual, he also break's God's laws of love and, consequently, sins against God. Confession must be made to both parties.

True confession contains several elements: a value judgment, sorrow, and forgiveness. The tax collector in the parable of the Pharisee and the publican evidenced all three elements.

> But the tax collector, standing far off, would not even lift up his eyes to heaven, but beat his breast, saying, "God, be merciful to me a sinner!" I tell you, this man went down to his house justified, rather than the other (Luke 18:13, 14a).

First, then, a value judgment must be made by the child or young person concerning his own conduct. The criteria to be used are the commandments of love: love God and love your neighbor. The child is to look at his behavior in a critical manner and judge it on the basis of whether he believes that it was in responsive obedience to God, whether it was for his own welfare, and whether it demonstrated concern for others. The child must personally make such a value judgment to decide whether or not his behavior was acceptable or unacceptable against those criteria. It is obvious because of the confrontation that the adult views the behavior as being unacceptable, but true confession must include personal acknowledgment of guilt. If the child is unwilling to make such a value judgment (no one is unable), then there is little the teacher can do to help the child at that point. Natural and logical consequences for the unacceptable behavior must follow. There is no avoiding the consequences for one's actions by not owning up to personal culpability for them. But the adult must not give up. He must continually ask for a value judgment by the child concerning his behavior.

Such admission of wrongdoing is necessary before sorrow can be accepted as being genuine and for forgiveness to take place. Forgiveness can, indeed, be offered, but personal accepting of guilt and demonstrating sorrow for one's actions are prerequisites for the acceptance of pardon. If a child refuses to admit that his conduct was wrong, most times it will be out of stubbornness or rebellion. But there is the possibility that he is not familiar with the criteria through lack of instruction, or he is not committed to those criteria as guides for his own life. If this is true, then nurture (both instruction and correction) and prayer for a heart change are probably the wisest actions that a teacher can take at that point.

There is an additional problem which may be encountered. A child or young person may indeed be committed to Jesus Christ and to the norms contained in Scripture, but he may interpret the scriptural directives in a way that is different from that of the teacher. This is legitimate, up to a point. The point comes when the child or young person disobeys the rules of the school. The failure to obey such rules must be acknowledged by the child, but this can be done without having to state agreement with them. Compliance with the established rules of a school is a necessary part of biblical obedience to those placed in authority.

The making of such a value judgment on the part of the child is to be followed by sorrow or repentance. It is one thing to admit guilt, but it is quite another thing to be sorry for it. This is a difficult factor to deal with. A teacher cannot force a child to be sorry for what he has done. He is either sorry or he is not! Hebrews 12:16, 17 speaks of Esau, who was not sorry for his actions but the consequences of his actions. That, too, is unacceptable. True sorrow can best be evidenced in changed behavior. Repeating Proverbs 28:13: ". . . he who confesses and forsakes [transgressions] will obtain mercy."

Certain habits and patterns of conduct often have to be broken or changed at this point. This can appear to be humanly impossible. But the Lord is able and promises the power of the Holy Spirit to assist. Persons who rely on God in such a way experience a very thrilling dimension of the Christian life.

Sorrow or repentance is to be followed by forgiveness. Luke 17: 3, 4 states:

> Take heed to yourselves; if your brother sins, rebuke him, and if he repents, forgive him; and if he sins against you seven times in the day, and turns to you seven times, and says, "I repent," you must forgive him.

The number "seven" represents "completeness" (i.e., every time). There is no limit on forgiveness. A person must always be ready to grant forgiveness when true sorrow is evidenced. That is why the issue of love which was stressed under the topic of confrontation is so important. Each child needs at least one adult who will *always* be there and will *never* give up on him. This is not only a human need for healing to take place, it is a biblical injunction. This is the type of love which Christ demonstrated and requires of Christian teachers. They must go to the student where he is at, accept him as he is, and then never give up on him. (Perhaps the human inadequacy to perform such a task struck the disciples, because the verse directly following the ones quoted above reads: "The apostles said to the Lord, 'Increase our faith!' ")

### Covenanting

Confrontation and confession are to be followed by covenanting, joining together in a commitment for the future. Covenanting includes several activities—gathering information, determining options, and making a plan that is agreeable to both parties.

The first step toward planning for a redirected form of behavior is information gathering. The teacher must attempt to obtain all information that relates to the conduct of the child. It would be helpful for the adult involved to begin this process *before* the point of confrontation and the discussion which follows. If the problem is a consistent one, the teacher has time for this more systematic approach. If not, he may have to rely on memory and known facts. This information should be assimilated in a file so that the pieces of information can be viewed together. It is likely that certain pieces may begin to fit together in some type of logical pattern of relationships.

The gathering of such information can begin with observing the child. Since the conduct of individuals is purposive and goalistic, this viewing of the child's behavior can often provide insight into his goals, attitudes, and expectations. It is helpful to observe a child under various circumstances as well. It can be beneficial for a teacher to be invited to the home of one of his students, not necessarily for the fine meal which might be served, but to observe the conduct of the child at home and the relationship between parents and the child. Conduct at home, while playing in the neighborhood or on the playground, and in the classroom should be observed so that insight can be gained into patterns of behavior, incongruity of behavior under varying circumstances, and the goals, attitudes, and expectations of the child. A noble goal of any observation is to "get to know" a person better. An interesting exercise toward this end is to write a biographical sketch of a person simply from information gathered through observation. There is one caution, however, to be mentioned at this point. Although there is some valid rationale for objectivity and scientific analysis, the child must always be viewed as a person, not as an object.

Information gathering should also include the collecting of data for what could be called a case study. This case study should include information about the family, church, and social life of the child. It should also include information on school achievement, past behavior patterns, and the like. Although biblical admonition does not accept the deterministic approach to behavior which the behavioral psychologists Freud and Skinner might advocate, it is probable that there were factors which did *influence* the child's behavior. It is important to gather as much data as possible so that effective planning for corrective actions can take place.

The next step in information gathering is to try to recognize the goals of the child. There is evidence which indicates that the purposes for the disturbing behavior of elementary school-age children can usually be broken down into the following four categories:

1. *Desiring attention*
   — by being a nuisance (active form)
   — by laziness (passive form)
2. *Questing after power and superiority*
   — through rebelliousness (active form)
   — through stubbornness (passive form)
3. *Seeking revenge*
   — through viciousness (active form)
   — through passivity (passive form)
4. *Accepting real or imagined inadequacy* through an attitude and demonstration of hopelessness

These goals are actually substitute goals for more acceptable ones which the child, for whatever the reason, believes that he cannot achieve or desires that he should not achieve. For instance, a child who feels unable to achieve social acceptance through acceptable means might act on the faulty logic that his misbehavior will give him the social acceptance he desires. He may believe that status and a sense of personal value is more easily obtained through useless and destructive means than through more appropriate and acceptable actions.

There is much evidence that a great amount of human behavior is a result of man's desire to feel lovable and to be loved. He wishes to have a positive self-image and self-confidence based on a sense of proficiency and competence. He also wishes to be accepted as part of his peer group. These goals are of real importance for children of elementary school age. Young people in high school, on the other hand, often seem to view status and excitement as their most highly esteemed values and, consequently, the purpose underlying much of their behavior. The sad fact of the matter is that so many children and young people seek these goals in an unscriptural, abnormal manner. The goals of a positive self-image, social acceptance, status, and excitement are not wrong in themselves. They become wrong when God is not acknowledged as the source and reason for such goals.

Teachers should make an attempt to recognize the child's goals. The following are three possible ways to verify whether or not one is on target.
1.  Observe the child and simply attempt to match the behavior with one of the four goals listed.
2.  Analyze one's spontaneous reaction to the child's misconduct.
    — If one feels *annoyed,* this would indicate a desire for attention, goal one.
    — If one feels *defeated* or *threatened,* this would indicate a quest after power or superiority, goal two.
    — If one feels deeply *hurt,* this would indicate a seeking of revenge, goal three.
    — If one feels *helpless,* this would indicate an acceptance of inadequacy, goal four.

3. The third means is through the child's responses to correction. It is extremely important that the teacher does not immediately do what he feels like doing. That would simply tend to reinforce the student's behavior. It is usually best to do the opposite of one's first impulse. This corrective feedback should give some indication whether or not the assessment was accurate. Briefly, the reactions of the teacher could be as follows:

*Goal 1.* Do not give the attention the child desires simply upon demand. Give attention at other times when it is not being demanded.

*Goal 2.* Do not fight back. Fighting violates respect for the child. But do not give in either. Giving in violates respect for oneself.

*Goal 3.* Do not communicate hurt, either verbally or non-verbally. Rather, convince by actions (turn the other cheek) that he is liked.

*Goal 4.* Give encouragement when he makes mistakes. Emphasize what the child does correctly.

4. The fourth means is helping the child to become aware of his motivations. Simply telling a child to behave is often futile—he already knows that he should. But explaining the purpose behind his behavior can give him the insight necessary for a change of goals and thus a change in behavior.

The teacher should approach the student in a very low-keyed manner and ask him if he knows why he misbehaved. Usually the student will answer "no." The teacher can then ask whether the student might be interested in hearing a few ideas that he has. He should ask all of the following questions, since the student may have more than one goal.

— Could it be that you want attention?

— Could it be that you want your own way and hope to be boss?

— Could it be that you want to hurt others as much as you are hurt by them?

— Could it be that you want to be left alone?

The child may not answer with a verbal "yes" or "no," but he will usually demonstrate a *recognition reflex* when the question accurately reflects his goal. Once this bit of honesty is shared beween the student and the teacher, progress can be made toward establishing new goals.

\* \* \* \* \*

There are other forms of behavior that reflect the child's inability to reach goals which are very important to him. These terms would not normally be used with children, but the concepts themselves may prove to be helpful.

Sometimes a thwarting object or person can come between a child and his goal and make it difficult or impossible for the child to reach his goal. Biblically, there are several actions suggested. One should first look at the goal to determine its worth. Perhaps the Lord is "closing the door" on that particular goal. Assuming, however, that the goal seems to be within the Lord's will, one should pray for the guidance and strength either to work through the obstacle or to work around it. Working within difficult circumstances can help a child develop a Christian maturity through increased reliance on the Lord.

But often a child does not follow biblical directives, and his actions may reflect other choices on his part, choices of which he may not be consciously aware. *One,* he may aggressively fight the thwarting object or person which is standing in the way of him reaching his goal. If for some reason he cannot or is afraid to fight, he may use *displacement* to rid himself of his feelings of frustration. This means that he will switch his aggressive feelings and actions from the original source to some other person or object. The story goes of the man who, after being soundly "chewed out" by his boss, went home and kicked his poor, unsuspecting dog. That would be displacement in action. Scapegoating—blaming others for one's failures or actions— is also a form of displacement and a major source of prejudice.

A *second* type of reaction to the thwarting of the reaching of a goal could be the acceptance of a *substitute* or *alternate* goal. That, within a biblical framework, may be exactly the right thing to do. Recognizing one's abilities and one's limitations is quite acceptable. But the defense mechanisms which may accompany such a move are not always as acceptable, since they can reflect dishonesty with one's self. Rationalization is very common. Other persons are given socially acceptable "reasons" for one's failures or actions. Identification is another such defense mechanism, one less harmful if it is understood and accepted. One "identifies" with others who have been successful in reaching the goal which was personally sought. If empathetic happiness over the success of others can overcome personal envy, identification can have merit. But one should not live his life through others. God desires a unique response from his unique creatures. A third defense mechanism is compensation. This occurs when a person becomes an "overachiever" in one area in an attempt to offset a "failure" to achieve a more desired goal. Young people who have difficulty with the academic side of school may "bury" themselves in athletics. The reverse can also be true.

A *third* reaction to the thwarting of a personal goal is that of *withdrawal*. One form is physical withdrawal. A person drops out or quits. He is no longer willing to fight what appears to be insurmountable obstacles to achieve what he desires. A second form of withdrawal is fantasy. A bit of fantasy is probably a healthy thing, but some children withdraw too much into books, movies, daydreams, and the like. The obstacles to reaching life's goals become so large and so painful that the child begins living in an imaginary world in which he finds success and does not encounter pain. As was mentioned, a bit of fantasy, a bit of withdrawal through imagination, can be quite refreshing. But when fantasy begins to envelop a major portion of the child's time, he is not coping with life's realities as he should.

Children and young people have purpose in their actions. They are attempting to achieve certain personal goals. If a child has behavior problems, the teacher should seek a better understanding of these goals. A child who cannot reach a goal through acceptable and appropriate means may use unacceptable and inappropriate means. Some of these involve others; some involve only one's self. An adult who possesses insight into reasons for particular conduct can and should assist a child with self-understanding.

*      *      *      *      *

Scripture speaks about the importance of *listening*.

If one gives answer before he hears, it is his folly and shame (Prov. 18:13).

Know this, my beloved brethren. Let every man be quick to hear, slow to speak, slow to anger . . . (James 1:19).

Perhaps the most fruitful means of collecting information is through *actively listening* to the child or young person. Listening to children can help resolve problems in several ways:

1.  It helps to get *all* of the information out where it can be dealt with.
2.  It helps to get at the *real* problem if there happens to be one at a less obvious level.
3.  It helps the person to *see* his own problem more clearly, and this assists him in solving it by himself.

Active listening differs from passive listening in one important way. The adult who does the listening attempts to paraphrase back to the child what he hears the child saying. This type of paraphrasing can accomplish two purposes: One, it can determine whether the adult is operating on the same wave length as the child. Inaccurate paraphrasing will force the child to say it in another way; it could also lead to frustration if the "wave length" continues to be different. The adult should then retreat into a noncommittal grunt or nod of the head. Secondly, correct paraphrasing sends the message to the child that "I know where you're at," and, in essence, encourages the person to keep talking. The more a child can be encouraged to talk without the interference of suggestions or ideas, the more the likelihood that pertinent information will be shared.

Active listening involves listening for the *content* of the message first of all. The child should be encouraged to continue talking until all of the information is out on the table. This must be done without the interference of adult judgment, suggestions, or ideas. But active listening also involves listening for *feelings* which may or may not agree with the content. At times the feelings that are expressed betray a more serious problem at a much deeper level. So, it is important as an active listener to be able to "hear what a person is saying" *and* to "sense how he is feeling." If that empathetic type of genuine concern can be felt by the child, the child will be more prone to be open in expressing his innermost thoughts and concerns. It is good for a teacher to try to "get into the skin of the child" so that he can view life and the world in the same manner as the child.

This type of active listening helps one to understand the inner attitude of the child. For the Christian the *why*, or motive, behind the act is more important than the act itself. The story is told of two bricklayers, both of whom were doing identical work on a structure. One, when asked what he was doing, replied, "Laying bricks." The second, when asked what he was doing, replied, "Building a cathedral." The first workman was viewing his work on a horizontal plane. The second viewed his work on a vertical plane, doing *all* to the glory of God. Motives and attitudes are crucial within a biblical framework of counseling. Only by demonstrating sincere interest in a person and by listening perceptively can one gain meaningful insight into that aspect of a person's behavior.

Finally, active listening can help a person solve his own problem. The aim of counseling is not to create dependence or even to have an adult solve a problem for a child or young person. Ideally, the child should be guided toward personal insight and the ability to come up with possible solutions to the problem himself. Self-understanding, self-acceptance, and self-direction are three goals of biblical counseling—all within a context, however, of self-surrender to Jesus Christ.

After information gathering, the second step toward planning for a redirected form of behavior in the future is *determining options*. This activity, also called brainstorming, involves thinking of as many solutions to the problem as possible. No judgment is made at first of the practicality or worth of a suggestion. Allowing such a non-judgmental activity to take place can help the child to feel free to express his ideas. It is amazing how often a child can think of a solution which the teacher did not think of or was afraid to suggest. Emphasis should be placed on the child doing the brainstorming. After all, the problem is his and it would be healthy if he could come up with his own solutions as well. That is not always possible, and the adult might have to offer a few suggestions, too. The suggestions should be written on a chalkboard or on some other area visible to both parties, so that all possibilities can be viewed when the priorities have to be arranged.

Gathering information and determining options are followed, finally, by *making a plan of action.* The possible actions that were listed should be placed in a hierarchy of priorities. The final selection of the plan of action should be made by the child or young person. But the plan must be agreeable to all parties involved, and it must be in harmony with biblical norms and the goals of the school.

Once the plan of action is agreed upon by both parties, they should covenant with each other to implement the agreed upon solution to the problem. This covenant involves commitment on the part of both the teacher and the child. Both are committed to each other and to the plan upon which they mutually agreed. To prevent misunderstanding and to emphasize this commitment, it would be helpful if the plan were written out and signed by both parties.

## Summary and Conclusions

Biblical correction (restorative action) must always be supplemented by biblical counseling (restorative communication). The amount of counseling necessary depends on the situation and the child. The goals of counseling are reconciliation and restoration. The child is to experience a healing of relationships, and he is to accept anew the place and the task God has for him. These goals are reached by way of a three-stage admonishing process. First, there must be confrontation, so that the child can become aware of the unacceptability of his conduct. Secondly, there must be confession, an action which includes a value judgment, sorrow, and forgiveness. Thirdly, there is covenanting. This includes the gathering of information, the determining of options, and the making of and commitment to a plan of action.

Once again, this process must take place within the context of genuine love, acceptance, and respect. Such a relationship *must* be felt by the child if he is to trust the teacher. Counseling is not the act of giving advice. Counseling involves getting to know the child and then assisting the child to make personal and responsible decisions about his future attitudes and conduct.

The counseling process is never carried out in textbook fashion. Life and people are never quite that predictable. The details of the process will differ with each situation and with each person. But there are certain principles of which an adult should be aware, so that the goals of biblical counseling can be sought and, Lord willing, can also be reached.

# Afterword

## The Teacher

Lord, who am I to teach the way
To little children day by day,
So prone myself to go astray?

I teach them knowledge, but I know
How faint they flicker and how low
The candles of my knowledge glow.

I teach them power to will and do,
But only now to learn anew
My own great weakness through and through.

I teach them love for all mankind
And all God's creatures, but I find
My love comes lagging far behind.

Lord, if their guide I still must be,
O, let the little children see
Their teacher leaning hard on THEE.
                    —Leslie Pinckney Hill

That prayer no doubt accurately expresses the feelings of many
teachers who, after reading this book, feel overwhelmed by the
enormity and complexity of the task before them. Some may have
feelings of discouragement and despair. Most probably feel inadequate as they seek to nurture God's children.

These feelings are not unusual. Most of us who work with children experience these feelings at various times. These feelings have

a certain legitimate quality to them. After all, isn't it true that people who really care about children also recognize how inadequate they are to really meet the needs of their children? And the more they care, the more rapidly they come to that realization.

The danger, however, comes if we were to dwell on these feelings of discouragement and inadequacy to the point of giving up. That would be in conflict with God's desires for us. You see, God wants us to be totally dependent on him. Moments of despair can be used to force us from our attitude of self-sufficiency down to our knees in dependency. That is the beauty and comfort of being a Christian teacher. God does not expect us to nurture his children by ourselves. The words of II Corinthians 12:9 state: "My grace is sufficient for you, for my power is made perfect in weakness." God delights in using finite humans so that his power and glory can be known. Paul recognizes this as he says, ". . . it is no longer I who live, but Christ who lives in me; and the life I now live in the flesh I live by faith in the Son of God, who loved me and gave himself for me" (Gal. 2:20).

Scripture provides many examples of God taking people who felt inadequate for a task and using them so that it would be obvious that he was the source, not they. Moses was one such person.

> But Moses said to the LORD, "Oh my Lord, I am not elo-quent, either heretofore or since thou hast spoken to thy servant; but I am slow of speech and of tongue." Then the LORD said to him, "Who has made man's mouth? Who makes him dumb, or deaf, or seeing, or blind? Is it not I, the LORD? Now therefore go, and I will be with your mouth and teach you what you shall speak (Ex. 4:10-12).

Gideon also questioned God about his capabilities:

> And he said to him, "Pray, LORD, how can I deliver Israel? Behold, my clan is the weakest in Manasseh, and I am the least in my family." And the LORD said to him, "But I will be with you, and you shall smite the Midianites as one man" (Judges 6:15, 16).

I Samuel 16 records the process of selecting a replacement for Saul as king. Rather than choosing one of the older, apparently more capable sons of Jesse, Samuel chose David the shepherd, the youngest. For, as God explained to Samuel, "Do not look on his appearance or on the height of his stature . . . for the LORD sees not as man sees; man looks on the outward appearance, but the LORD looks on the heart" (vs. 7).

Christ himself chose twelve very unlikely prospects to serve as his disciples, men who later "turned the world upside down" (Acts 17:6). He does the same today. Christian teachers are called by God to a task for which he provides the strength and direction. His grace is sufficient.

God provides many means for hope and encouragement. Christian teachers are to seek his face in prayer. We are to remember that God does not depend on us but we on him. He is able to carry out his divine will without us, but he provides us with the blessed opportunity to be instruments in this process. Our prayer life must be continual and vibrant. Praying for one's children on a daily basis is the most powerful tool available in the process of nurturing children in the Lord. There is a saying that when our children are young we should talk to them about Jesus; when our children are older we should talk to Jesus about them. There are times with older children that we as teachers can *only* pray for them; all other avenues appear to be closed. The prayer of a righteous man or woman continues to have "great power in its effects" (James 5:16).

Christian teachers are also to search the Scriptures daily for direction. The book you have just read has been written by a finite man; it does not replace Scripture. Measure its truthfulness against God's Word. Accept only what you believe to be in harmony with the Bible. Do not practice any concepts in this book unless you believe them to be true, based on God's Word. Understand what you believe. Do not follow the suggestions of this book blindly. Understanding will allow for a personal application of the principles suggested. Each child and each circumstance is unique and must be dealt with in a unique fashion—within certain broad guidelines. That is the reason this book is intended to be a *study,* not a hand book. No one can write a book that covers all possible situations in life. Broad concepts or principles must be understood, accepted, and then applied on an individual basis. These principles must be in harmony with Scripture. And the only way to determine that is to personally search the Scriptures daily.

A book like this can have the tendency to overwhelm a person. Where does one begin to apply the principles it contains? The answer is to begin exactly where you and your children are right now. Do not attempt to understand or apply all of the principles at once. That would be an impossible task. Take one step at a time. Move slowly but surely. Neither you nor your children can probably handle a radical departure from past patterns. Determine the need and then plan steps that will put you on the right course. Growth in teaching is a lifelong process. One never really arrives.

Do not compare your situation with others. Measure the growth taking place in your classroom against your own past experiences. Each classroom is unique—and so are you. We are not meant to be alike. Each person and each classroom is given unique potential and unique responsibility to develop that potential for God's glory. Comparison with others simply does not fit the realities of the situation. The questions must be: Is there growth? Is there progress?

The ideas in this book should be integrated with the person of the teacher. Each of us possesses a unique personality. Remain true to who you are. Persons operating from common principles often carry out the implications of those principles in differing ways. That is to be expected, since they are different personalities. There is no one *best* way to nurture children in the Lord. We, our children, and the circumstances in which we are placed differ considerably. There are certain principles based on Scripture which provide direction for all. But the application of those principles can and should vary.

Not only do we have strength from God and the freedom to function as individuals, but we also have the Christian community from which to draw assistance. I Corinthians 12 speaks of the members of the body caring for each other, a theme echoed in I Timothy 5. All members of the body of Christ, his church, have responsibilities toward each other. It is true that parents are primarily responsible for the nurturing of their children, but other members of the Christian community are to assist in this endeavor in whatever way they can. Christian teachers and parents should not feel or operate in isolation.

They should seek guidance and support from their brothers and sisters in Christ.

Mistakes will be made. Sometimes one step backward will be taken for two steps forward. Be willing to admit and accept mistakes. There are no perfect teachers around. Base what you believe on the Bible; then step out in faith and act on your beliefs. Stepping out in faith means that the consequences of your actions may not always be known in advance. But simple obedience is what God expects from us. As sovereign God he is always in control. He can correct our mistakes. He can change our minuses into pluses. Weakness through Christ becomes strength. All he asks is a heart commitment that is directed toward him and actions which are based on that heart commitment. He promises to honor, bless, and sanctify such actions.

# Glossary of Terms

ABSOLUTE DEPRAVITY. The view that each act of man is 100 percent sinful, with no "redeeming" features whatsoever. (*See* TOTAL DEPRAVITY for a contrast.)

ACHIEVEMENT MOTIVATION. The anticipatory motivation that comes with being able to complete a project, to see what one has created or produced.

BEHAVIORISM. A view of man and his behavior which states that environmental factors *cause* people to behave in a particular manner. People are viewed as *reactors*. Thus if a teacher seeks a change in a student's behavior, the desired behavior must be positively reinforced (rewarded). In other words, if good things (from the viewpoint of the child) happen after certain actions, the student will want to continue doing those actions. Such an approach to discipline is called "behavior modification." B. F. Skinner is considered to be the "father" of behavioral psychology.

CAUSISTIC. The theory that behavior is caused by factors outside of the individual, i.e., environment. *See* BEHAVIORISM.

CHASTEN. To correct or redirect someone; a forward-looking action.

CIVIL GOOD. Just actions; those of a legal, legislative, or judicial nature, done for the welfare of others.

COMMANDMENTS OF LOVE. Jesus' injunction in Matthew 22:37-39 to love (obey) God and to love (show concern for) one's neighbor; also referred to as the great commandments or the laws of love.

COMMEND. The act of commenting on or pointing out what one has done well. This is in contrast to the form of praise which places a moral label upon a person as being "good" because he has done something well. The former is instructive and promotes independence; the latter often promotes dependence.

COMPETENCE MOTIVATION. The motivation that comes with being able to do something for oneself; the joy in having a part or say-so in the process.

CORPORAL PUNISHMENT. Used in the traditional sense this would include spanking or paddling a child's bottom; physical punishment.

CULTURAL MANDATE. The task given by God to man at the dawn of creation—to uncover and develop creation's potential for God's glory and man's welfare; first mentioned in Genesis 1:28.

DETERMINISM. The theory that (adult) behavior is predetermined by activities and relationships which occurred during early childhood, with a focus on those early childhood activities that have a sexual context. A theory developed by Sigmund Freud.

DISCIPLINE. The unified act of instructing and correcting; nurture.

EMIT. A voluntary response by an individual. This is in opposition to an "elicited" response, one that is either drawn out by another or is in reaction to a stimulus outside of one's self.

ENVIRONMENTAL PERCEPTION. The act of perceiving the factors within one's physical environment as well as within one's psychological environment. The latter may include factors within one's memory and imagination. Perception takes place through the use of the five senses—and, perhaps, through the "sixth sense" of intuition as well.

GESTALT. An integrated structure forming a whole unit; configuration; pattern. A word of German origin.

GOALISTIC. Establishing a goal and seeking to reach or achieve that goal. In opposition to being "causistic" or "deterministic."

GREAT COMMISSION. Part of man's God-given task—to disciple the nations. This directive by Jesus is found in Matthew 28:19-20.

HIERARCHY OF NEEDS. The motivational theory of the late Abraham Maslow which states that man acts to meet his basic needs—first his "deficiency" needs and, once these have been met, his "higher being" needs.

HUMANISM. A man-centered philosophy of life. In this sense, behaviorism can be considered to be humanistic. But there are two more precise meanings. Historically, the term *humanism* referred to the humanities. As the liberal arts were considered to be the vehicle for liberating man, so the humanities were seen as the avenue for understanding the fulness of man's humanity. More recently humanism has come to mean humaneness or humanitarianism. People are viewed as having inner direction and goal orientation. They are *actors* rather than *re*actors. Two leaders within humanistic psychology are the late Abraham Maslow and Carl Rogers. Behaviorism and humanism are the two dominant themes within psychology and education today.

IMAGE-BEARER. According to Scripture (Gen. 1:27), man bears the image of God. The *static* dimension of bearing the image of God is evidenced in certain characteristics of man which reflect God (e.g., creativity). The *dynamic* dimension of bearing the image of God is evidenced in man's serving as God's representative or ambassador within his creation (e.g., stewardship; caring for the needy).

I-THOU RELATIONSHIP. Treating another in a respectful manner, as a person—one who brings something of dignity and worth to the relationship—rather than as an object to be acted upon or manipulated.

KING. One who rules; one who provides service through dominion. Part of the office of man.

LEGALISM. Obeying the letter of the law while ignoring the spirit of the law; the rule or law becomes an end in itself.

LOGICAL CONSEQUENCES. Those consequences of an action which are imposed by an outside source and are designed to logically fit the misdeed.

MORAL GOOD. Kind actions toward another; helpful acts.

NATURAL CONSEQUENCES. Those consequences of an action which take place without outside interference.

NATURAL GOOD. Natural actions which contribute to one's temporal welfare, such as walking and talking.

NATURAL REVELATION. The revelation of God—the Creator—through creation. Also called general revelation.

NURTURE. The unified act of instructing and correcting; discipline.

PERSONS-OF-SIGNIFICANCE. The important people in one's life, those whose opinions and reactions greatly affect the forming of one's self-image.

PRIEST. One who mediates, brings healing; part of the office of man.

PROPHET. One who informs, speaks the truth; part of the office of man.

PURPOSIVE. Having a purpose; forward looking. As opposed to causistic and deterministic.

RESTRAINING PRESENCE, GOD'S. The act of God restraining the growth and impact of sin in the world, so that his divine purposes can come to pass; also called "common grace."

SELF-FULFILLING PROPHECY. The theory that if one treats another person in a particular manner (e.g., capable, bright, stupid, talented) he will begin viewing himself as being that type of person and will act accordingly.

SELF-PERCEPTION. How one views and feels about himself; self-image; self-concept.

SPECIAL REVELATION. The written revelation of God through his Word, the Bible.

SPIRITUAL GOOD. Those actions which are done in obedience to God and for his glory; those actions which are presented perfect to God the Father by Jesus the Son, who serves as Mediator of the redeemed in him.

TOTAL DEPRAVITY. The view that each act of man contains the taint of sin—a sinful inclination.

TUNNEL VISION. Narrowed perception caused by a sense of threat; only the "threatening" object or person is perceived.

# Bibliography

Ackerman, J. M. *Operant Conditioning Techniques for the Classroom Teacher.* Glenview, Ill.: Scot Foresman, 1972.

Adams, J. E. *Competent to Counsel.* Nutley, N. J.: Presbyterian and Reformed, 1970.

————. *Godliness Through Discipline.* Nutley, N. J.: Presbyterian and Reformed, 1972.

————. *The Christian Counselor's Manual.* Nutley, N. J.: Presbyterian and Reformed, 1973.

Allport, G. W. *Becoming.* New Haven: Yale University Press, 1965.

Anderson, C. *Phi Chi.* Unpublished manuscript. Covenant College, 1974.

Baruch, D. *How to Discipline Your Children.* New York: Public Affairs Pamphlets, 1973.

Berkhof, L. *Systematic Theology.* Grand Rapids: Eerdmans, 1941.

Berkhouwer, G. C. *Man: The Image of God.* Grand Rapids: Eerdmans, 1962.

Beversluis, N. H. *Christian Philosophy of Education.* Grand Rapids: National Union of Christian Schools, 1971.

Biehler, R. F. *Psychology Applied to Teaching.* 2nd ed. Boston: Houghton Mifflin, 1974.

Bigge, M. L. *Learning Theories for Teachers.* 2nd ed. New York: Harper & Row, 1971.

Bramblet, J. M. *Christian Ethics.* Whittier, Calif.: California Association of Christian Schools, 1974.

Bright, R. L., and Vincent, J. J. "JACS: A Behavior Modification Program That Works." *Phi Delta Kappan* 55(1973):17-19.

Brown, D. *Changing Student Behavior: A New Approach to Discipline.* Dubuque: Brown, 1971.

Brunner, J. S. *The Process of Education.* New York: Vintage, 1960.

————. *Toward a Theory of Instruction.* Cambridge: Harvard University Press, 1966.

Buber, H. *I and Thou.* 2nd ed. New York: Scribner's, 1958.

Carrison, M. P. "The Perils of Behavior Mod." *Phi Delta Kappan* 55(1973):593-595.

Case, R. "Piaget's Theory of Child Development and Its Implications." *Phi Delta Kappan* 55(1973):20-25.

Christenson, L. *The Christian Family.* Minneapolis: Bethany Fellowship, 1970.

Clarizio, H. F. *Toward Positive Classroom Discipline.* New York: Wiley, 1971.

Combs, A. W. *The Professional Education of Teachers.* 2nd ed. Boston: Allyn & Bacon, 1974.

Covenant College. *Statement of Purpose.* Lookout Mountain, Tenn.: Author, 1974.

Craig, R. "Lawrence Kohlberg and Moral Development: Some Reflections." *Educational Theory* 24 (1974):121-129.

DeBoer, P. P. "A Case for Informal Education in Christian Schools." *Christian Educators Journal* 14(1974):24-30.

DeJong, N. *Education in the Truth.* Nutley, N. J.: Presbyterian and Reformed, 1969.

DeWaal, S. C. J. "A Scriptural Model of the Learner." Paper presented at the meeting of the Association of Christian School Administrators, Sioux Center, Iowa, August, 1972.

————. "The Humanization of Education." Paper presented at the meeting of the Midwest, Christian Teachers Association, Chicago, October, 1972.

Dobson, J. *Dare to Discipline.* Wheaton, Ill.: Tyndale, 1970.

Dreikurs, R. *Psychology in the Classroom.* 2nd ed. New York: Harper & Row, 1968.

Dreikurs, R.; Grunwald, B. B.; and Pepper, F. C. *Maintaining Sanity in the Classroom.* New York: Harper & Row, 1971.

Dreikurs, R., and Cassel, P. *Discipline Without Tears.* New York: Hawthorn Books, 1972.

Elam, S., ed. *The Gallup Polls of Attitudes Toward Education 1969–1973.* Bloomington, Ind.: Phi Delta Kappa, 1973.

Ellison, C. W. "Christianity and Psychology: Contradictory or Complementary?" Reprint from *Journal of the American Scientific Affiliation,* Elgin, Ill.

Ernest, K. *Games Students Play.* Millbrae, Calif.: Celestial Arts, 1972.

Fennema, J. "Behavior Modification: A Wolf in Sheep's Clothing." *Christian Home and School* 52(1973):16-17.

———. "Thou Shalt Love Thyself." *Christian Home and School* 53 (1974):12-14.

———. "Students as Image Bearers: It Makes a Difference." *Christian Educators Journal* 14(1975):14-15.

———. "Covenant Children and Attitude Change: What Are the Responsibilities of the Christian School?" *Christian Educators Journal* 15(1976):19-22.

Fennema, J., and Stouwie, R. "Some Thoughts on Christian Faith and Behavior Modification." *Christian Home and School* 54 (1976):6-7, 12-15.

Gaebelein, F. E. *The Pattern of God's Truth.* Chicago: Moody, 1968.

Gazda, G. M. *Human Relations Development.* Boston: Allyn & Bacon, 1973.

General Assembly of the Presbyterian Church in the United States. *The Confession of Faith.* Richmond: Author, 1965.

Ginott, H. *Teacher and Child*. New York: Macmillan, 1972.

Glasser, W. *Reality Therapy*. New York: Harper & Row, 1965.

———. *Schools Without Failure*. New York: Harper & Row, 1969.

———. *The Identity Society*. New York: Harper & Row, 1972.

———. "A New Look at Discipline." *Learning* 3(1974):6-11.

Gnagey, W. J. *Controlling Classroom Behavior*. Washington, D. C.: National Education Association, 1965.

———. *The Psychology of Discipline in the Classroom*. New York: Macmillan, 1968.

Gordon, T. *Parent Effectiveness Training*. New York: Wyden, 1970.

Greene, J. *Discipline as Self-direction*. Washington, D. C.: National Education Association.

Hart, H. H. *Summerhill: For and Against*. New York: Hart, 1970.

Hitt, W. O. "Two Models of Man. *American Psychologist* 24 (1969):651-658.

Hoekema, A. A. *The Christian Looks at Himself*. Grand Rapids: Eerdmans, 1975.

Holt, J. *Freedom and Beyond*. New York: Dell, 1972.

Holt, J.; Ginott, H.; Salk, L.; and Barr, D. "Discipline: The Most Perplexing Subject of All." *Teacher* 90(1972):54-56.

Holtrop, P. "Sheep with a Name." Reprint from *Eastern Christian School Herald*, 1972.

Jaarsma, C. *The Educational Philosophy of Herman Bavinck*. Grand Rapids: Eerdmans, 1935.

———. *Human Development, Learning and Teaching*. Grand Rapids: Eerdmans, 1961.

Kienel, P. A. *The Christian School: Why It Is Right for Your Child*. Wheaton, Ill.: Victor, 1974.

Kounin, J. S.: *Discipline and Group Management in Classrooms*. New York: Holt, 1970.

Krumboltz, J. D., and Krumboltz, H. B. *Changing Children's Behavior.* Englewood Cliffs, N. J.: Prentice-Hall, 1972.

Lee, F. N. *The Origin and Destiny of Man.* Nutley, N. J.: Presbyterian and Reformed, 1974.

Lindsey, B. L., and Cunningham, J. W. "Behavior Modification: Some Doubts and Dangers." *Phi Delta Kappan* 54(1973):596-597.

Long, G. W. "Fathers That Function." Sermon presented at the Lookout Mountain Presbyterian Church, Lookout Mountain, Tenn., June 16, 1974.

Lovett, C. S. *What's a Parent to Do?* Baldwin Park, Calif.: Personal Christianity, 1971.

Madsen, C. H., Jr., and Madsen, C. K. *Teaching/Discipline.* 2nd ed. Boston: Allyn & Bacon, 1974.

Madsen, C. K. "Values Versus Techniques: An Analysis of Behavior Modification." *Phi Delta Kappan* 54(1973):598-601.

Madsen, C. K., and Madsen, C. H., Jr. *Parents/Children/Discipline.* Boston: Allyn & Bacon, 1972.

Martin, A. "Scriptural Principles and Their Application for Training of Children." Paper presented at the meeting of the Mid-Atlantic Christian Schools Association, Atlantic City, November, 1974.

Maslow, A. H. *Toward a Psychology of Being.* 2nd ed. New York: D. Van Nostrand, 1968.

————. *The Farther Reaches of Human Nature.* New York: Viking Press, 1971.

May, P. *Which Way to Educate?* Chicago: Moody, 1975.

Milhollan, F., and Forisha, B. E. *From Skinner to Rogers.* Lincoln, Nebr.: Professional Educators, 1972.

Miller, K. *The Becomers.* Waco, Tex.: Word Books, 1973.

Moustakas, C. *The Authentic Teacher.* Cambridge: Doyle, 1966.

Narramore, B. *Help! I'm a Parent.* Grand Rapids: Zondervan, 1972.

————. *An Ounce of Prevention.* Grand Rapids: Zondervan, 1973.

Narramore, B., and Counts, B. *Guilt and Freedom.* Santa Ana, Calif.: Vision House, 1974.

Narramore, C. M. *Discipline in the Christian Home.* Grand Rapids: Zondervan, 1961.

National Education Association. *Report on the Task Force on Corporal Punishment.* Washington, D. C.: Author, 1972.

Nation's Schools. "It's Time to Hang Up the Hickory Stick." Author, 90(1972):8-9.

Nazigian, A. *Teach Them Diligently.* Brookhaven, Pa.: The Christian Academy, 1974.

Nederhood, J. "The Trouble with the Family." *The Radio Pulpit* 17 (1972):15-24.

Neill, A. S. *Summerhill.* New York: Hart, 1960.

————. *Freedom—Not License!* New York: Hart, 1966.

Niebuhr, R. *The Nature and Destiny of Man.* New York: Scribner's, 1941.

Nuermberger, R. M. "The Nature of Man and Guilt: Implications for Counseling Derived from an Analysis of the Philosophies of Cornelius Van Til and Erich Fromm." Unpublished doctoral dissertation, Michigan State University, 1967.

O'Leary, K. D., and O'Leary, S. C. *Classroom Management.* New York: Pergamon, 1972.

Pearson, C. *Resolving Classroom Conflict.* Palo Alto, Calif.: Education Today, 1974.

Pepper, W. F. *The Self-Managed Child.* New York: Harper & Row, 1973.

Persons, S. *Toomer Log: A Blow by Blow Description of Applying Positive Reinforcement.* Atlanta: Project Success Environment, 1973.

Pine Rest Christian Hospital. *Parent Enrichment Program, Instructors Manual.* Cutlerville, Mich.: Author, n.d.

Pittenger, O. E., and Gooding, C. T. *Learning Theories in Educational Practice.* New York: Wiley, 1971.

Reitman, A.; Follman, J.; and Ladd, E. T. *Corporal Punishment in the Public Schools.* New York: American Civil Liberties Union, 1972.

Roberts, D. E. *Psychotherapy and a Christian View of Man.* New York: Scribner's, 1950.

Rogers, C. R. *Freedom to Learn.* Columbus, Ohio: Merrill, 1969.

Runner, H. E. *The Relation of the Bible to Learning.* Toronto: Wedge, n.d.

Sapp, A. C. "Succeeding with Success Environment." *American Education* 9(1973):4-10.

Schaeffer, E. *Christianity Is Jewish.* Wheaton, Ill.: Tyndale, 1975.

———. *What Is a Family?* Old Tappan, N. J.: Revell, 1975.

Schaeffer, F. A. *Back to Freedom and Dignity.* Downers Grove, Ill.: Inter-Varsity, 1972.

Schouls, P. A. *Insight, Authority and Power: A Biblical Appraisal.* Toronto: Wedge, 1972.

Seerveld, C. *Cultural Objectives for the Christian Teacher.* Palos Heights, Ill.: Trinity College, n.d.

Sheviakov, G. V., and Redl, F. *Discipline for Today's Children and Youth.* Washington, D. C.: National Education Association, 1956.

Silberman, C. E. *Crisis in the Classroom.* New York: Random House, 1970.

Skinner, B. F. *Beyond Freedom and Dignity.* New York: Knopf, 1971.

———. "The Free and Happy Student." *Phi Delta Kappan* 55 (1973):13-16.

———. *About Behaviorism.* New York: Knopf, 1974.

Snygg, D., and Combs, A. W. *Individual Behavior*. New York: Harper, 1949.

Steensma, G. J. "Meaningful Learning." Signal Mountain, Tenn.: Signal, 1971.

――――. *To Those Who Teach*. Signal Mountain, Tenn.: Signal 1971.

Stoops, E., and King-Stoops, J. *Discipline or Disaster?* Bloomington, Ind.: The Phi Delta Kappan Educational Foundation, 1972.

Stouwie, R. "Deceiver or Molder?" *Christian Home and School* 53 (1974):18-19.

Todd, K. R. P. *Promoting Mental Health in the Classroom*. Washington, D. C.: U. S. Government Printing Office, 1973.

VanBrummelen, H. "Discipline unto Discipleship." *Christian Home and School* 53(1975):6-8.

Van Til, C. *Common Grace*. Nutley, N. J.: Presbyterian and Reformed, 1954.

――――. *Essays on Christian Education*. Nutley, N. J.: Presbyterian and Reformed, 1974.

Vos, C. *Biblical Perspectives on Authority*. Grand Rapids: Calvin College, 1974.

Vriend, J. *To Prod the "Slumbering Giant."* Toronto: Wedge, 1972.

Wann, T. W. *Behaviorism and Phenomenology*. Chicago: The University of Chicago Press, 1964.

Waterink, J. *Basic Concepts in Christian Pedagogy*. Grand Rapids: Eerdmans, 1954.

Watson, L. S., Jr. *Child Behavior Modification*. New York: Pergamon, 1973.

Wiener, D. N. *Classroom Management and Discipline*. Itasca, Ill. Peacock, 1972.

Zylstra, H. *Testament of Vision*. Grand Rapids: Eerdmans, 1958.